D1521663

Kant for Everyman

Kant after a drawing by Püttrich

KANT

FOR EVERYMAN

by

WILLIBALD KLINKE

Translated from the German by
MICHAEL BULLOCK

LONDON

ROUTLEDGE AND KEGAN PAUL

Kant for Everyman
First published in England 1951
by Routledge and Kegan Paul Ltd
68-74 Carter Lane London E.C.4
and printed in Great Britain
by Latimer Trend & Co Ltd Plymouth
Published in German in 1949
by S. Hirzel Verlag, Zurich
as Kant für Jedermann

Foreword

THIS BOOK is intended for readers of good general education, but, as is clear from its title, it lays no claim to making any new contribution to the knowledge of Kant already possessed by specialist students of philosophy. I have confined myself to the aim of familiarizing a wider public with the ideas of this sometimes difficult philosopher, by presenting them in a more easily comprehensible form.

The prime difficulty in approaching this thinker lies in Kant's tendency to exclusively abstract expression, and the infrequency with which he illustrates his ideas by examples. A philosopher so thoroughly at home in the highest regions of abstract intellectual reflection, could have no feeling for the difficulties involved in comprehending his system of thought, in consequence, apart from anything else, of the form he chose for its presentation. I have limited my exposition to his main ideas and have not dealt with secondary, specialized problems. *Critique of Judgement*, the work of his old age, which is undoubtedly to be numbered amongst his major works, has intentionally been omitted from consideration, not only because it would be out of place in a book intended for 'everyman', but also because its implication is far removed from that of the rest of his basic writings.

In order not to confuse the reader without special training in philosophy, and so that he should not overlook what is essential in Kant's philosophical outlook, I have confined critical comment on the material under discussion within the limits imposed by my particular purpose.

If this exposition succeeds in awakening interest in Kant's system of ideas, and in stimulating the reader to its further study, for which a wealth of literature is available, its aim will have been achieved.

Zürich,   DR. WILLIBALD KLINKE
July 1949

Contents

9

CONTENTS

Illustrations

LIFE AND ACTIVITIES

I

Early Environment

IMMANUEL KANT, the fourth child of the master harness-maker,[1] Johann Georg Kant, was born in Königsberg on the 22nd April 1724.

Königsberg, at that time, was a city of considerable importance with some 50,000 inhabitants. In later years, the philosopher commended it as one of the centres of the country's political and intellectual life and, since it was a seaport whose population included many Eastern races, as a place well suited to the development of a knowledge of the world and mankind. Being the capital of the Duchy of Prussia, and the seat of a university (Collegium Albertinum, founded 1544), Königsberg was the most important cultural centre of Eastern Germany. Kant felt indebted to his native town for his pronounced interest in the peoples and countries of the world, and his especial predilection for geography, of which he possessed a detailed knowledge.

Kant's father, an upright citizen and an honest craftsman, brought up the nine children, with which his wife Anna Regina Reuter, the daughter of a fellow-craftsman from Nürnberg, had presented him in twenty-two years of marriage (of whom four met an early death), to industry and truthfulness. He had married in the year 1715, when he himself was approaching thirty-three and his wife was only eighteen. Kant's mother died in 1737, when he was only thirteen years old, and he lost his father in 1746. His parents lived in very humble circumstances, but were not so poor as to go short of essentials or be oppressed by want. They earned just so much as they needed for their domestic existence and the upbringing of their children, though only by very modest standards.

[1] At that time the Guilds differentiated between harness-makers and saddlers.

Throughout his life, Kant thought of his mother, a tranquil god-fearing woman, with no other aim in life than the loyal fulfilment of her duty to her family, with the most sincere respect. In his judgment, she was possessed of great natural intelligence, a noble heart, and genuine piety devoid of all trace of mysticism. Whenever he spoke of her it was with emotion, and his eyes glistened. The image of his mother was deeply impressed upon him; it had a decisive effect on his conception of life and mode of living. 'I shall never forget my mother,' he once remarked to his friend Jachmann,[1] 'for she planted and tended the first seeds of good in me. She opened my heart to the impressions of nature; she awakened and widened my ideas, and her teachings have had an enduring, healing influence on my life.'

She seems to have bestowed her mother-love particularly freely upon this son, of whose receptiveness she was well aware. She frequently accompanied her little Immanuel out into the country and drew his attention to the objects and phenomena of nature; she even talked to him, within the limits of her own knowledge, about the structure of the heavens, and was again and again astonished by his quick intelligence and power of understanding. Many of her bright son's questions found her at a loss for an answer.

The peace, tranquillity and order which reigned in his parents' house exercised a beneficial influence on Kant's development and upbringing. When advanced in years, he still proclaimed that, morally speaking, his parents—both of whom were models of uprightness and moral virtue and, though without fortune, had left no debts behind them—had given him an upbringing which could not have been bettered.

His parents were godly people and Pietists; this religious movement found expression in their whole conduct of life. In later years, when he subscribed to different views on religion, Kant still stated as his opinion: 'Whatever may be said about Pietism,

---

[1] Jachmann, Reinhold Bernhard, Director of the Provincial School and Institute of Education at Königsberg, one of the earliest of Kant's biographers. (*Immanuel Kant, as seen through letters to a friend.* Königsberg, 1804.) Letter 8, p. 99 f.

Kant, a painting by Döbler, 1791

Kant, after an oil-painting by Becker, 1768

it is enough that those in whom it was an earnest belief were distinguished by their praiseworthy conduct. They possessed the highest good known to man, that tranquillity, that joy, that inner peace, which no passion can disturb. No misery, no persecution dismayed them, no controversy was capable of provoking them to anger or enmity. In a word: even the mere onlooker was compelled to involuntary admiration.'[1] Although his mother's deep piety was free from any fanaticism, her care for the spiritual well-being of her children nevertheless led to the establishment of special hours for prayers, to which she adhered strictly and which made a deep impression on the young Immanuel.

2

In the Collegium Fredericianum
(1732–40)

THE YOUNG KANT was given his first lessons in the elementary school attached to St. George's Hospital, an institution for the aged. This school, in which reading, writing, some arithmetic and 'Christianity' were taught, was presided over by a single teacher, who was also leader of the choir and organist. Kant was to spend only a few years there. Continually surprised by her boy's intellectual alertness, his mother decided that, as soon as it were possible, he should enjoy a better education. The opportunity was soon to present itself. She was a regular attendant at the prayer and bible meetings of Dr. Franz Albert Schultz,[2] a much respected leader of the Pietists, who had come to Königsberg as preacher at the Old City Church. He became Kant's mother's moral counsellor, was a frequent visitor to the

---

[1] Rink: *Scenes from the Life of Kant.* Königsberg, 1805, p. 13.
[2] Schultz, F. A., preacher and member of the consistory council (1692–1763.)

family and thus made the acquaintance of little Immanuel and his exceptional abilities and unusual gifts. He advised the boy's mother to introduce him to the study of theology, which was the fulfilment of her heart's desire. This decision simultaneously determined the choice of college, so at Easter, 1732, the eight-year-old entered the Collegium Fredericianum, of which Schultz himself became Director the following year. He attended this institution until he left for the University in 1740.

The goal of the Protestant colleges of the time was, alongside instruction in Christianity, facility in the oral and written use of Latin, to which sixteen to twenty hours were devoted each week. The aim here was much more the inculcation of the ex-ternals of the language, than an introduction to the spirit of antiquity. At the beginning of his seventieth year, Kant wrote on a loose sheet of paper: 'Would to God that at school we had learnt the spirit and not the "phrases" of the authors, and had not copied them; our German writings would then have contained more genuine taste.'[1]

The pupils were trained, by unceasing practice, and the strict application of all the rules of grammatical method, to write Latin and even, up to a point, to speak it. The treastises which Kant wrote in Latin bear witness to the attainment of this educa-tional goal in his case.

Quick-wittedness and an exceptionally good memory made progress at school an easy matter for Kant, all the more so because his home background had accustomed him to diligence and con-scientiousness. For the rest, what the school had to offer in the way of general education was somewhat meagre; Kant, as he later remarked, regarded his greatest gain as having been his love for the old poets. Even in his old age, Kant was still able to recite long passages from the Latin classics, without prompt-ing.

The Fredericianum was strongly Pietist in character; it was popularly known as the 'Pietist school'. Every period began and ended with a 'short but edifying prayer'. For the boarders, an early morning service of half an hour's duration was held every

[1] *Complete Works of Kant*, Academy Edition, vol. xv, no. 778.

day; to these were added two further hours of devotion and prayer weekly, regular catechism at the hands of the Director, and a Saturday service of one hour. On Sundays there was a morning and an afternoon sermon, on the contents of which questions were asked in the evening. The excess of such performances was bound to make the pupils disgusted with religion. Kant himself later spoke contemptuously of such exaggerated ways of exercising a religious influence, using the phrases: 'Conglomeration of imposed pious observances' and the 'yoke of statutory ecclesiastical law' in contrast to the 'free moral service of God'.

Such an insupportable superfluity of services and devotional exercises turned piety into bigotry, and blunted religious feeling instead of developing it. Kant, who lived, not in the Collegium, but at home, had no very pleasant memories of the Fredericianum; he later told his friend Hippel,[1] that looking back on that enslavement of youth filled him with terror and dread. Hence, he would never have considered accepting a teaching post at that school; he had suffered too much under the oppression of this godly institution and its Pietist spirit. There is a remarkable passage in a letter written to him on the 10th March 1771, by his former schoolfellow, David Ruhnken[2] of Leiden, a famous philologist, which runs as follows: 'Thirty years have passed since the two of us groaned beneath the pedantically gloomy, but not entirely worthless discipline of those fanatics. At that time your intellectual capacities were generally held in the highest esteem. If you strove on with unabated zeal, you could attain to the most elevated realms of science.'

Kant completed his studies at the Fredericianum at the end of the summer of 1740. It was not usual at that time to set any particular examinations at the end of the pupils' studies, or to provide them with leaving certificates.

Before Kant had even finished his schooling, his deeply revered mother, who had contracted a fatal illness while selflessly tending a friend, died. It was a heavy blow for her son, who had

---

[1] Hippel, Theodor Gottlieb von (1741-96), author, 1780 Burgomaster and Chief of Police at Könisgberg.

[2] Ruhnken, David (1723-98).

been attached to her by a combination of the highest esteem and childlike tenderness.

The already modest circumstances of Kant's father deteriorated after the death of his mother; but a maternal uncle named Richter, a prosperous master shoemaker, took charge of his promising nephew and supported him as long as his studies continued, so that he was not hampered by any material difficulties.

3

At the University
(1740-46)

IN AUTUMN 1740, before he had reached his seventeenth birthday, Kant became a student at the University of his native town. At that time Königsberg enjoyed no particular reputation in the sciences. The universities of the period were instructional rather than research institutes and, in the main, textbooks were merely interpreted from the chair. Situated in an out of the way Protestant province, the University's primary task was the training of teachers and preachers. 'Königsberg is better suited', observed Crown Prince Frederick, on the occasion of a visit to the city in the year 1739, 'to the training of bears than to becoming a theatre of the sciences.'

Kant, as was the usual practice, began his studies in the faculty of philosophy,[1] which was then little more than a preparatory institution for the three higher faculties. Here the Latin school's instruction in language and literature was supplemented and extended by a course in the general or philosophical sciences.

[1] The faculty of philosophy developed from the medieval faculty of 'arts', in which were practised the seven free arts, the *'artes liberales'*, namely grammar (Latin), dialectics and rhetoric (the *trivium*, or threefold path), and arithmetic, geometry, music (theory) and astronomy (the *quadrivium*, or fourfold path).

Since Kant had left home, in order no longer to be a burden on his father, he would have been entitled to free board and lodging in the residence which existed for students without means. But he preferred to keep his freedom, and shared a simple room with another student. He earned his living by coaching less gifted, but more well-to-do students. As he was used to living very simply and frugally, he was able to devote himself to his studies, undistracted by want. But he could not participate in the various students' antics, which were then usual, though no longer so to-day; in any case, such activities would not have been in conformity with his serious conception of life. One of his few recreations consisted in playing billiards, at which he showed great skill and which, when played for money, provided him with an occasional source of income. Amongst his close friends he was regarded as such a formidable champion that he could never find a challenger. But a new source of income was presented to him by the current passion for playing ombre,[1] at which he soon became a master and which then became of considerable assistance to him.

Kant had worked out his own curriculum. He had no intention of devoting himself to theology or following the profession of preacher; the excess of religious instruction had left him with an antipathy towards this domain of study. Above all, his interest was captured by philosophy, the natural sciences and mathematics. These sciences were taught by the still young lecturer Martin Knutzen (1713–51), to whom Kant felt particularly attracted, with whom he entered into a more personal relationship and who placed books from his library at Kant's disposal. Martin Knutzen acquainted him with the philosophy of Christian Wolff,[2] which was then in vogue, and introduced him to mathematics and physics. Kant's study of mathematics was of the greatest importance to his subsequent philosophic thought; for mathematics brings unhesitating conviction of the existence of

[1] A card game invented by the Spaniards. The name is derived from the Spanish word *hombre*, man.

[2] Wolff (really Wolf), Christian, Freiherr von (1679–1754), founder of the philosophical system of Rationalism or Enlightenment.

absolute truth, and demonstrates how far we can proceed with cognition, independently of experience. Throughout his life, Kant felt a particular predilection for the study of the natural sciences and, even in his old age, his favourite reading for mental relaxation consisted in works on geography.

It is probable that Kant left the University and his native city in the second half of 1747, partly as the result of external circumstances. His father had died on the 24th March 1746, leaving no property whatever; he received a 'pauper's' burial at public cost. So nothing further bound the young scholar, now in his twenty-third year, to Königsberg. His plan of becoming a recognized university teacher, i.e. of commencing his academic career as a private docent, had to be postponed, since he was entirely without means and therefore wished first to earn a living and accumulate some savings. He is one of those important people who achieved everything by their own efforts. At that time, the path for those without funds generally passed through the stage of being a private tutor.

4

Kant as a Private Tutor
(1747–54)

KANT was forced to spend no less than seven long years as a private tutor, before he was finally able to embark on his academic career. He hoped that this position would not only enable him to earn a living and amass some small savings, but that it would also leave him enough spare time to prepare for his future teaching post and carry on his scientific work.

At that period there were few public secondary schools in East Prussia, so that the landed gentry and occasionally even well-to-do country clergy had to turn to a private tutor for the upbringing and education of their sons.

In summer 1747 the twenty-three-years-old Kant entered the household of Pastor Andertsch in the Lithuanian village of Judtschen, which lies between Insterburg and Gumbinnen. This minister was of Silesian origin and officiated in the local Reformed Church community, largely composed of peasants from French Switzerland, who had settled there after Lithuania had been decimated by the plague which ravaged it during the years 1709-11.[1] The pastor had five sons, of whom the youngest were to receive their schooling from Kant; the two eldest were already attending the Joachimsthal Grammar School near Berlin. Kant remained with this family three years, but little is known of his stay.

Kant's second private tutorship was with the titled landowner Bernhard Friedrich von Hülsen at Gross-Arnsdorf near Saalfeld, where he was entrusted with the education of the three eldest sons, aged respectively thirteen, ten and six. Here again he passed some years, before returning in 1754 to Königsberg, where he remained until his death. The simple, secluded life in these two lonely places had enabled the extremely thrifty Kant to save up enough to begin thinking of the realization of his plan of life, of embarking on an academic career.

There can be no doubt that Kant did his duty in these two positions in an irreproachable manner, but it is hardly likely that he can have derived much pleasure from the exercise of this profession. In his modesty, he later frankly confessed to his friends at table that 'probably, there was never in this world a worse private tutor than he, and that the business of a pedagogue had always seemed to him one of the most unpleasant'. It is easy to imagine that it must have been difficult for Kant, with his pronounced tendency to abstraction, to put his instruction into such a concrete and elementary form as to be easily understood by young children. But he was, nevertheless, highly esteemed in the

[1] The plague, which had been brought into the country from Poland, had destroyed 236,000 people—a third of the population. To replace the loss, Frederick William I did everything in his power to promote immigration.

two families, and one of Hülsen's sons later became a resident pupil in Kant's house. The eldest of these three pupils had received such good preparation that he was able to go straight into the highest class of the famous Joachimsthal Grammar School, whose standards were high.

Kant's activities as a teacher provided him with a rich source of experience, upon which he drew freely in his subsequent lectures on education. They also enabled him to make social contacts and acquire an air of good breeding, which he kept for the rest of his life. He hated 'paying compliments' and the frequent exaggerations of conventional politeness, but nevertheless, in all his later copious social relations as teacher and author, he never ceased to remain, in speech and writing, the well-bred man who is always master of himself. His experiences as a teacher were, therefore, of the greatest value to him in his subsequently extensive social intercourse.

His studies and scientific work had made such progress during the period of his private tutorships that, by the 17th April 1755, he was able to present to the University his thesis (written in Latin) for the degree of Doctor or, as it was then called, Magister. It was a natural philosophic treatise entitled *De Igne*, 'Concerning Fire'. He sat the oral examination shortly after and, on the 12th June 1755, the degree of Doctor was solemnly conferred on him by the Dean of the Faculty.

On this occasion, as was usual, he delivered a speech in Latin, taking as his subject: 'The Simpler and more Fundamental Exposition of Philosophy.' The learned and eminent public, which was present at this ceremony, listened with the greatest attention to the promising young docent's dissertation. His formal recognition by the University as a reader in mathematics, physics and philosophy took place in the autumn of the same year, and with it began the future philosopher's academic career.

5

Years as a 'Magister'
(1755–70)

KANT commenced his activities as a 'magister' at the age of thirty-three; this period passed quietly, with little outward eventfulness. But he had to possess his soul in patience for fifteen years, before he succeeded in obtaining a chair at the University. He was passed over twice; he also turned down many invitations from elsewhere, because he clung to the hope of eventually finding a satisfactory position in his native town, to which he was deeply attached. He kept his goal firmly before his eyes. 'I shall follow my course, and nothing shall deflect me from it,' he stated. He insisted upon 'subordinating things to himself, not himself to things'. But he wanted to attain the cherished post of Professor of Philosophy at the University by his own merits; nothing was further from his mind than to forge his career by influence and connections.

At the beginning of his academic activity his lectures, besides logic and metaphysics, dealt primarily with mathematics and the natural sciences. One important subject, which also aroused great interest outside the ranks of his regular students and brought him many listeners, was 'physical geography'. Under this heading, he provided an orientation in the most valuable facts from the realms of nature and man. In consequence of the wide number of disciplines which fell within his province, he used to give sixteen lectures a week; but sometimes these lectures took up twenty-six to twenty-eight hours a week—a tremendous schedule of work! In spite of this, he found time to publish numerous scientific works, of which one is especially worthy of mention, *General Natural History and Theory of the Heavens, or an Attempt to Explain the Composition and Mechanical Origin of the*

Universe on Newtonian Principles (1755). The book is dedicated to Frederick II and first appeared anonymously. As the publisher went bankrupt, it passed almost unnoticed to begin with.

Kant's aim in this work was to explain the structure of the universe, and in particular the stellar system, genetically on the basis of mechanical laws. The Frenchman, Laplace,[1] though unaware of the existence of Kant's paper, later developed similar ideas as to the genesis of the stellar system from a 'primal nebula' in his work, *Exposition du système du monde*, published in 1796. Hence, this is known to-day as the Kant-Laplace theory.

Kant intended this work to be a popular exposition and, therefore, dispensed with any mathematical proofs. It is, in fact, an imaginative, ingenious and bold hypothesis concerning the genesis of the world, which is admittedly contradicted by many astronomical facts and physical laws and leaves numerous circumstances in the world of the heavenly bodies unexplained. That Kant himself valued this treatise particularly highly, however, is clear from the fact that he came back to it again and again, even after several years, and recalled its basic thesis by means of extracts.

As a private docent, Kant's financial position was not altogether unfavourable, as the result of his tireless industry and thrift. In the early years, he gave board and lodging to wealthy students. Although Königsberg was a somewhat poorly attended provincial university, Kant's lectures were never short of listeners; since he rapidly acquired a reputation for great erudition. From 1758 to 1762, Königsberg fell under Russian occupation; it thus happened that Kant frequently had the opportunity of giving private lessons in mathematics to Russian officers.[2]

At his request, he obtained in 1766 the vacant position of assistant librarian of the Royal Library, which brought with it a

[1] Laplace, Pierre-Simon, Marquis de (1749–1827), mathematician and astronomer. His major work was *Mécanique céleste* (5 vols, 1799–1825). His theory on the genesis of the planetary system is contained in *Exposition du système du monde* (2 vols., 1796).

[2] Under Frederick the Great, Prussia was occupied by the Russians, following the battle of Grossjägersdorf (30th August 1757), and remained in their possession from 1758 to 1762.

salary of 65 Taler. In addition, he was for a considerable time in charge of a private natural-history and art collection, which induced him to study mineralogy. His income was therefore sufficient for his modest needs. Even as a magister he had been able to run a household comprising two rooms, a manservant and a maid. He had saved twenty golden crowns, which he put aside as a protection against total destitution in the event of illness. He therefore had no need to write for gain, as many others did, and his publications always arose from an inner need.

The Königsberg of that day had precious little to offer in the way of social life. A small circle of acquaintances used to meet now and then for a 'peasant supper' at the Trutenau Windmill inn, on the outskirts of the town. Kant was no lover of noisy pleasures, he valued most the 'quiet gaiety of the mind'. His preference was for the society of people outside his own special field, of educated men of the most varied walks of life. The young Kant, the magister, did not yet lead such a pedantically regulated life as the professor was to do later.

At the end of the morning lecture, he liked to betake himself to a coffee-house for a cup of tea or coffee, and to play billiards, which he had learnt to enjoy in his student days. His midday meal he took out, when not privately invited—as he often was. He occasionally went out in the evening as well, to play ombre in a tavern or in private society. He considered this game a useful exercise of the intelligence, and also in self-control, as well as being the only thing capable of diverting his mind from strenuous thought. Later, he gave up card-playing entirely, for one reason because his fellow-players were too slow for him, and for another because he preferred to take part in conversation. Since Königsberg possessed a theatre from 1755 on, he sometimes used to attend a play or a concert; but no matter how late he came home, he invariably rose early.

As long as he was firm on his feet, he also liked going for excursions into the country surrounding his native town. He frequently put up at the Moditten forester's house, situated about a mile north-east of Königsberg in the midst of the forest; here he entered into terms of close friendship with Head Forester

Wobser. 'The latter was just the host he wanted for a stay in the country,' reports Borowski,[1] 'free from any trace of artificiality in expression or manners, of very fine natural intelligence and a noble and kind heart. He used to stay with him during the academic vacations, and even through the whole week.'

It was in these charming surroundings that, in 1764, he wrote the pamphlet (intended for a more general public): *Observations on the Sentiment of the Beautiful and the Sublime*. The idyllic place in which this work was written may have contributed to the fact that it contains an almost poetic language, to which we are not accustomed in the sober, abstract philosopher, as for instance, when he writes of 'tall oaks and solitary shadows within the holy grove', and of 'flower-filled meadows and dales with winding streams, the peaceful stillness of a summer's eve, when the tremulous light of the stars breaks through the night's brown shadows, and the lonely moon stands on the horizon' and so on.[2]

Even in his younger days as a magister, Kant sought in his place of residence, above all, quiet in respect both of the house and its surroundings. Thus, he moved out of his rooms in Magister Street, which ran alongside the Pregel, because the noise of the ships and the Polish vessels disturbed him. Towards the middle of the year 1760, he was living with the bookseller and publisher Kanter in the fine-looking Guildhall, where he had rented the left half of the second story and where he also held his lectures. 'At the beginning of September 1768,' recounts Vorländer,[3] 'Kanter opened up a new shop, above the entrance to which a huge Prussian eagle spread its mighty pinions. In no time, this shop was as lively and cheerful as a literary coffee-house. Anyone arriving there in a stage coach from home or abroad towards eleven in the morning was confronted with a bustle of activity. The latest publications on the book market were spread out on a large table for anyone interested to look at. Together with the latest political papers, they were available to every visitor—and, on two days of the week, also to students—

[1] Borowski, Ludwig Ernst (1740-1831). Königsberg Town Pastor.
[2] *Collected Works of Kant*, Academy Edition, Berlin, 1905, vol. ii, p. 208 f.
[3] Vorländer, Karl: *Immanuel Kant*, Leipzig, 1924, vol. i, p. 182 ff.

for free reading. Professors of the University and other men of learning used to gather at this literary meeting-place, partly to gather information and partly, also, to pass a few moments in stimulating conversation. These visitors carried on discussions, wrote their letters in Kanter's counting-house, organized collections for various purposes, and sometimes even assisted in serving customers. The busy bookseller's lodger, the "noble" Magister and later Professor Kant, must often have made his appearance in the shop: of small stature—not above five feet tall —and slight build, which yet bore a mighty head with a wide brow, shining blue eyes and a fresh complexion. He would have been carrying his three-cornered hat in his hand, so that the little fair-haired and white-powdered wig together with the hair-bag, which often slipped over from the slightly raised right shoulder towards the left, were in full view; round his neck he would have been wearing a black cravat, while on his breast the finely folded ruffle could be seen between the brown or variegated black, brown and yellow cloth of his coat and waistcoat; for in his view, which he frequently put forward in his lectures as well, these colours formed a harmony. According to the fashion of the day, the waistcoat reached down to below his hips; to this were attached knickerbockers of the same colour, reaching to the knees, and to these grey silk stockings and shoes adorned with silver buckles. His sword, with its embroidered ribbon, hung at his side; coat, waistcoat and knickerbockers were fastened with a golden cord, their buttons covered with silk.

Since the astute publisher allowed the now famous magister to take all the books he wanted into his own rooms, especially as they lived under one roof, the scholar in return gave him all his own writings for publication, to which this enterprising individual may more than once have persuaded him.'

Kant was, however, driven out of this house which he shared with Kanter and where he enjoyed living, by a neighbour who kept in the courtyard a cock, which used to disturb him with its crowing while he was at work. He wanted to buy this noisy creature from its owner at any price, for the sake of restoring quiet; but he was defeated in his purpose by the stubbornness of

the neighbour, who refused to believe that the cock could incon-
venience the scholar. Kant left his rooms with Kanter very un-
willingly, because the latter's business was so active as to enable
him to keep abreast of the latest appearances in the book-world
at the expense of very little time. After living for a short period
in the cattle-market and, shortly afterwards, near the Wooden
Gate, he moved into a little house with a garden, not far from
the Castle and in a fairly quiet neighbourhood, which his friend
Hippel, whom we have already mentioned, found for him at
the end of 1783. But even here he was not to remain undisturbed.
For the prison was situated in the vicinity; the vociferous choral
singing of the prisoners frequently disturbed him at his work,
especially in summer, when he opened the window of his study,
which lay on the side of his house nearest the gaol. His vigorous
protest to the municipal president concerning the 'stentorian
devotions of the hypocrites in prison', whose 'spiritual welfare
would hardly be endangered if they were to give voice behind
closed windows (and even then, without yelling with all the
power of their lungs)', met with success to the extent that the
convicts were ordered to indulge their love of singing behind
closed windows.

Kant suffered much annoyance through street-urchins repeatedly throwing stones into his little garden. His complaints
on this score were fruitless; he was informed by the police that
the culprits could not be punished, since neither he nor any of
his people had so far been injured or hurt by their activities. 'In
other words,' he once exclaimed indignantly, 'the law cannot
punish them till I am sick or dead.'

We have already mentioned in passing that Kant received and
rejected certain invitations. These were made during his last few
years as a magister. In the winter of 1769, he was offered the chair
of theoretical philosophy (logic and metaphysics) at the University of Erlangen, with a remuneration of five hundred Rhenish
Gulden, five cords of firewood and a travelling allowance of a
hundred Taler. Kant refused. He received the second offer in
January 1770, from Jena; but he would have nothing to do with
this either, as there now seemed to him to be good prospects of

a post to his taste falling vacant in Königsberg itself. And he was not mistaken. On the 31st March 1770, King Frederick II signed an order-in-council nominating Kant Professor-in-ordinary of logic and metaphysics in the Faculty of Philosophy of his native town. After fifteen years as a magister and valuable scientific work and teaching, Kant had finally attained his cherished goal.

A few years later, he was to be once more tempted to accept a post which would have greatly extended his sphere of activity. This came about in the following manner. Freiherr Karl Abraham von Zedlitz, Minister for Ecclesiastical and Educational Affairs in Berlin (1771–8), who had a high regard for Kant, was planning reform of the universities. In a letter of the 1st August 1778 to the scholar he held in such esteem, he wrote: 'Give me the means of keeping university students away from the "bread and butter" subjects and making it clear to them that the little bit of juris-prudence, and even theology and medicine, will be infinitely easier and its application far more sure for the students with a greater knowledge of philosophy, and that they will only be judges, lawyers, preachers or doctors for a few hours each day, while for so many hours they will be men, for which they will need quite different forms of knowledge; I want you to teach me how to make all this clear to the students.' Zedlitz intended to make available to Kant a wider sphere of activity, more in keeping with his significance than Königsberg. He proposed that he should accept a professorship at Halle, with a commencing salary of 600 Taler and a special allowance of 200 Taler. At Königsberg he received only 236 Taler. The Minister pointed out that it was Kant's duty 'to disseminate knowledge and light throughout a wider circle, for the common good'; he gave him hopes of the title of Councillor, and pointed out how much bet-ter the climate would be for him in the centre of Germany than on the Baltic coast; all in vain. Even the greatly increased salary did not serve to persuade Kant to accept the invitation. He re-mained true to his native town; for, as he wrote to his friend Marcus Herz,[1] 'private gain and public applause were no incen-tive' to him. He believed that, in refusing, he was following 'the

[1] Herz, Marcus (1747–1803), physician and philosopher in Berlin.

instinct of his nature'. 'All change frightens me.' Fate had already given him what he wanted: 'a peaceful situation, exactly suited to my needs, in which work, speculation and social contacts alternate with one another and my very easily affected, but otherwise carefree spirit, and my still more moody, though never sick body are kept busy without being over-exerted.' He therefore felt that he must heed this 'instinct of his nature', if he wanted to draw out to any length the threads of his life, which the Fates were spinning very thin and fine. For this reason, he requested his benefactor Zedlitz to do nothing to disturb his present happy state. It was thus the good fortune of the University of Königsberg to retain its important and world-famous scholar and research-worker till the end of his days.

6

Kant as a Professor

AFTER HIS APPOINTMENT as Professor-in-ordinary, Kant effected a reduction of his teaching hours, generally giving only two lectures a day and adding a third on Saturday for revision. He made no further increase in the scope of his lectures, apart from the fact that, in accordance with the current duties of a Professor-in-ordinary of the Faculty of Philosophy, he gave a lecture on pedagogy when it came to his turn to do so. Curtailment of his previously very extensive teaching activities was necessary, apart from any other reason, to give him more time for literary work on the completion of his philosophical system. For this purpose also, he gave up his post as assistant librarian in the Royal Library, which he had only taken in the first place to augment his rather small income. Before assuming his new position, Kant had to take his professor's oath, which, amongst other things, obliged him to acknowledge the Lutheran

Facsimile of Kant's handwriting

Kant's house

Church and foreswear dissenting sects, such as the Anabaptists and Zwinglians.

He carried on his lectures with model diligence, without any interruption from session to session. Jachmann, whom we have already mentioned, reports that throughout the nine years in which he was Kant's student, he could not remember a single occasion on which the latter had missed a period, or even been so much as a quarter of an hour late for one. 'He never read his lectures. During many periods he never even made use of a notebook, but had a few jottings in the margins of his textbooks,[1] which served him as a guide. He frequently brought no more than a tiny slip of paper into the lecture with him, on which he had outlined his ideas in a small, abbreviated hand.' In philosophy, his exposition of logic was the most easily understood. It was never Kant's intention to teach logic to his audience. He repeatedly asserted that what his students would learn from him was not philosophy, but how to philosophize, not merely thoughts to be repeated, but how to think. 'He was heartily averse to all uncritical repetition. Think for yourselves, inquire for yourselves, stand on your own feet, were expressions he was always using. He took pleasure in clarifying his students' uncertainties or explaining doubtful points in greater detail. His lectures frequently became open discussions, spiced with wit and good humour.'

His expositions often demanded very close attention for their understanding. He was not gifted with the ability to render the concepts and facts he was dealing with universally comprehensible, or of making them intelligible even to the inattentive listener, by repeating them in different words. He was not fond of note-taking. He could not bear to see important points neglected and unimportant ones carefully noted down.

'Even his teaching of metaphysics', his former pupil Jachmann informs us, 'was lucid and attractive. Kant had a particularly skilful method of asserting and defining metaphysical concepts, which consisted, to all appearances, in carrying out his inquiries in front of his audience; as though he himself had just begun to

[1] At that time, lectures were generally based on compendia and handbooks.

consider the question, gradually adding fresh determining concepts, improving bit by bit on previously established explanations, and finally arriving at a definitive conclusion of his treatment of the subject, which he had thoroughly examined and illuminated from every angle, having given the completely attentive listener not only a knowledge of the subject, but also an object lesson in methodical thought. Any student who had not grasped the course his lectures were accustomed to take, who straightaway accepted his first explanation as correct and final, simply amassed half-truths. But it frequently happened during these speculations that Kant, carried away by his own intellectual powers, pursued individual concepts too far, losing sight of the main subject in these digressions. On such occasions, he usually broke off suddenly with the phrase: "In short, gentlemen!" and rapidly came back to the central theme. Kant himself was well aware that his instruction in philosophy was not easy for the beginner, and openly encouraged students to prepare themselves for his lectures by attending those of another professor first.'

'Above all, my dear fellow,' writes Jachmann in letters to a friend, 'you should have heard his lectures on moral philosophy! In these he ceased to be merely a speculative philosopher and became, at the same time, a spirited orator, sweeping the heart and emotions along with him, as well as satisfying the intelligence. Indeed, it was a heavenly delight to hear his sublimely pure ethical doctrine delivered with such powerful philosophic eloquence from the lips of its very creator. How often he moved us to tears, how often he stirred our hearts to their depths, how often he lifted up our minds and emotions from the shackles of self-seeking eudaemonism[1] to the exalted self-awareness of pure free-will, to absolute obedience to the laws of reason and to the exalted sense of our duty to others! On these occasions, the immortal philosopher seemed to us to be inspired with a divine fervour and, in turn, he filled us with inspiration as we listened in wonder. His hearers cannot have left one of his ethics periods, without having become better men than when they went in.

[1] To Kant an 'eudaemonist' is an egoist, who takes expedience and his own happiness, not the idea of duty, as the highest determinant of his will.

'His principal aim in his lectures on rational theology was to contribute towards an intelligently enlightened attitude to religious matters; for this reason, he was always pleased to have a large number of theologians in his audience. On one occasion, this series of lectures was so poorly attended that he wished to abandon the course; but when he learnt that his limited audience consisted almost entirely of theologians, he delivered the lectures in spite of receiving only a small honorarium. He clung to the hope that these lectures, which he delivered with such lucidity and conviction, would spread the bright light of intelligent religious belief over the whole of his fatherland, and he was not mistaken; since many evangelists went forth from there and preached the gospel of the Kingdom of Reason.'

'His lectures on anthropology and physical geography, which also enjoyed the highest attendance, offered simpler but extremely attractive instruction. Here the exalted thinker was to be seen moving through the tangible world and illuminating man and nature with the torch of an original intelligence. His acute observations, which bore the stamp of a profound knowledge of the worlds both of men and of nature, were presented with such wit and originality, that all his hearers were delighted. It was a pleasure to see how adolescents found joy in the fresh vista on to man and nature which was opened up to them, while learned and experienced men of affairs sat beside them and also obtained an abundance of intellectual nourishment. In these lectures Kant was all things to all men, and it was perhaps through them that he made his greatest contribution to the common good.

'His lecture room was frequently too small to contain the whole of the large audience which attended his public lectures, so that many had to be content with the adjoining room or the entrance hall. Since Kant's voice was weak, absolute silence reigned among his students, so that even those at a distance might follow his words. Kant used to sit on a slightly raised dais with a low desk in front of him, over which he could look out into the room.

During his lectures he generally looked intently into the eyes of a not too distant student, and read in the latter's face the measure in which he was being understood. The least thing was capable of upsetting him, especially if it was something which disrupted a natural or established arrangement, which in turn disrupted the arrangement of his ideas.

'In one of his periods, his absent-mindedness struck me unusually forcibly. At the midday meal, Kant informed me that his thoughts had been continually interrupted by the fact that a button was missing from the coat of one of the students seated close to him. Involuntarily, his eyes kept returning to this gap and this had been the cause of his lack of concentration. He was equally distracted by any affectation of "genius" in the appearance of a student sitting near him, e.g. hair hanging loose over neck and brow, which was still unusual in those days, an open neck or the absence of a ruffle.

'His great virtues won Kant such admiration and respect as a professor, as can seldom have been enjoyed by an academic teacher. The proverb, "a prophet is not without honour, save in his own country", certainly did not apply to him. He was almost worshipped by his students, who took every opportunity of letting him know it. But he was himself a true friend of student youth. He took pleasure in the frankness, liberality and good-taste in nature and conduct, which distinguished the academic world from other social groups, and he disapproved of the way in which a few merchants' sons, who were studying, made a point of dressing, not like the other students, but like shop assistants. Hence, he took an active part in everything which had to do with the refinement of students' manners and general culture.

'He took the keenest pleasure in the diligence and good behaviour of adolescent students. The most certain way for a student to gain his approval, was to give proof of industry and attentiveness at the revision periods.' (Jachmann)

Herder has left us an admirable portrait of Kant the teacher at the height of his powers. Herder came to Königsberg at the age of eighteen, and studied with Kant from 1762 to 1764. He states in his *Letters on the Advancement of Humanity* (1793–7):[1] 'I had

---

[1] Kant allowed Herder, who was living in very straitened circumstances and had to earn his daily bread by teaching at the Collegium Fredericianum, to attend his lectures without payment.

the good fortune to make the acquaintance of a philosopher, who was my teacher. Though in the prime of life, he still had the joyful high spirits of a young man, which he kept, I believe, into extreme old age. His open brow, built for thought, was the seat of indestructible serenity and gladness. A wealth of ideas issued from his lips, jest and wit and good humour were at his bidding, and his instructional lecture was also the most fascinating entertainment.

'With the same esprit with which he examined Leibniz, Wolff, Baumgarten, Crusius and Hume, and analysed the laws of nature expounded by the physicists Kepler and Newton, he appraised the currently appearing writings of Rousseau, his *Emile* and his *Héloise*, as he did every fresh discovery in natural science which came to his notice, estimated their value and returned, as always, to an unbiased knowledge of nature and of the moral worth of man.

'The history of mankind, of nations and of nature, natural science, mathematics and his own experience were the wellsprings which animated his lectures and his everyday life. He was never indifferent to anything worth knowing. No intrigue, no sectional interests, no advantage, no desire for fame ever possessed the slightest power to counteract his extension and illumination of truth. He encouraged and gently compelled people to think for themselves; despotism was alien to his nature. This man, whom I name with the deepest gratitude and reverence, is Immanuel Kant; I recall his image with pleasure.'

At the age of sixty-two Kant, for the first time, became Rector of the University. He took office with solemn ceremony on the 23rd April 1786. The same morning a deputation of students brought their congratulations in a poem, one verse of which runs:

> Whose heart for honours never hungered,
> Nor felt the urge to satisfy base pride,
> Who in his daily life and actions
> Took his own holy ethics as a guide.

An eye-witness, the son of a colleague (Reusch), reported Kant's outward appearance on such solemn occasions:

'Even at an early stage in his career, people used to wait atten-
tively to see him as he crossed the courtyard of the Albertinum
on his way to the great lecture hall, for a meeting of the Senate,
or an academic ceremony, or the solemn handing over of the
new rectorate—the so-called rectoral election. He was always
very soberly dressed, and his deeply serious face, his head sunken
slightly to one side and his steady, but not too slow step attracted
respectful attention whenever he appeared. The light sand-colour
of his clothing, later replaced by dark brown, was unobtrusive:
light colours were then the fashion, black being reserved for
funerals and mourning. On warm days, as was then the custom,
he used to take off his hat and carry it on the gold knob of his
cane, leaving his head adorned by his finely powdered wig. Silk
stockings and shoes with buckles were also part of the usual cos-
tume of a well-dressed man in those days. . . . When, after the
ceremonial inauguration of the new Rector had been completed,
the latter, accompanied by the professors drawn up in faculties,
made his way to divine service in the Cathedral, Kant—when not
himself the Rector—was accustomed to walk past the church
door.'[1]

Kant, incidentally, felt his position as Rector to be nothing but
a burden; he was not in the least ambitious, and would gladly
have dispensed with such outward marks of recognition.

[1] Vorländer, II, 45 f.

7

Kant and Women

WOMEN PLAYED no great role in Kant's life; like many great philosophers, he remained a bachelor.[1] Had he thought of marriage there would have been no material obstacles, once he had been appointed professor— though by that time he was already forty-six. There can also be no doubt, according to Jachmann, that in his youth Kant had known love, 'for how could a man with such a warm heart for friendship have failed to experience also the warmth of love'? It is said that twice in his middle years he showed signs of a serious intention to marry. On the first occasion his thoughts turned to a gentle and beautiful widow, who had come to Königsberg to visit her relations. The second involved a pretty young girl, who was acting as lady-companion to a noblewoman with landed property in East Prussia. But he hesitated so long over making a proposal, being unable to bring his calculations as to the income and expenditure in his future household to a conclusion, that the first one, the widow, entered into matrimony with a man in the Prussian 'highlands', while the second, the young girl, left Königsberg with her mistress. From that time on Kant never again thought of marriage.[2] His poor physical constitution was no doubt also partly responsible for his lack of interest in mar-

[1] Schopenhauer, who likewise died a bachelor, once jokingly remarked that all the great philosophers had remained unmarried, for example Heraclitus, Democritus, Plato and Zeno, Descartes and Spinoza, Locke and Hume, Leibniz, and Kant. Socrates constituted an exception to the rule, but it certainly did not turn out well in his case.

[2] A nice novelistic version of this affair is given by Schricker in *From the Life of Immanuel Kant* in 'Art and Life, a new annual for the German home', Stuttgart, 1881, pp. 231–62. Republished by Hans Vaihinger, Leipzig, 1924.

riage plans. Added to this was the fact that, for years, poverty had precluded any idea of marriage. At seventy-five he is supposed to have remarked to a visitor, in jest: 'When I could have done with a wife, I wasn't in a position to support one, and when I was in a position to support one I had no further use for one.' He had no fundamental antipathy to marriage and often recommended it to younger friends. He valued and respected the fair sex and was of the opinion that contact with well-bred women gave 'polish'. But he would have nothing to do with 'bluestockings', and when his friend, the writer Hippel, discussed the emancipation of women in an anonymous pamphlet, *The Improvement of Women's Position in Society* (1792), he repudiated the whole idea. 'He would certainly have immediately turned his back on any female who had spoken to him of his *Critique of Pure Reason*, or endeavoured to draw him into a conversation on the French Revolution, which he was passionately fond of discussing in male society.' (Borowski) To an aristocratic lady who asserted that women were just as capable of acquiring learning as men, and that there really had been learned women, he made the rather tart rejoinder: 'Well, that's a matter of opinion.'

'Another time, when he had spoken at some length on the preparation of food, a worthy lady, who stood high in his esteem, said to him: "It really seems, dear Professor, as though you look upon us as nothing but cooks." It was a real pleasure to hear with what skill and refinement Kant propounded the view that a knowledge of cookery was the honour of every woman, and that by cheering and refreshing her husband when he sat down to table faint and fatigued by his morning's work, she was actually bringing cheer to her own heart in the form of lively conversation at table, etc.' (Borowski)

Kant himself attached importance to tasty food, and, on this account, was of the opinion that every girl, quite apart from her general education, should receive particular training for the vocation of housewife. Hence, he thought it just as desirable for a man to have his daughter taught the art of cooking by a cook as the art of music by a music teacher; for she would win far more respect and love from her future husband, whoever he

might be, whether scholar or man of business, by welcoming
him on his return from work with a tasty dish without music,
than with a tasteless one with music.

When advanced in years, Kant advised his younger friends
not to follow the dictates of passion in their plans for marriage,
but rather to let reason guide them in choosing a wife.

He was himself perfectly happy in celibacy and thought of
married life in the terms set out in the seventh chapter of the
First Epistle to the Corinthians. He agreed with the opinion of a
married woman of very sound judgment, who repeatedly said
to him: 'If you are all right as you are, stay that way!'

8

Social Life and Personal Appearance

ONE OF KANT'S most marked characteristics was his strong
feeling for friendship. Apart from Head Forester Wobser, whom we have already mentioned and in whose
forest-house he wrote his treatise on *The Sentiment of the Beautiful and the Sublime*, one of his closest and most trusted friends was
the English merchant Joseph Green (1727–86). According to
Jachmann's account this friendship arose at the time of the North
American War of Independence. One afternoon Kant went for
a walk in the Dänhof Gardens and came upon an acquaintance
in the company of some men in an arbour. He was drawn into
conversation with the latter and very soon the North American
War of Independence came under discussion. Kant espoused the
cause of the Americans, warmly defended its justice and gave
vent to some bitterness concerning the behaviour of the English. 'All at once, one of the company sprang up enraged, advanced upon Kant, announced that he was an Englishman,
asserted his whole nation and himself to have been insulted by

the latter's words and, with the greatest heat, demanded satisfaction in a bloody duel. Kant did not allow the man's anger to
disturb his composure in the slightest, but continued his conversation and commenced to outline his political principles and
opinions and the view that every man, without detriment to his
patriotism, should judge such world events as a citizen of the
world. So persuasive was his eloquence, that Green—for that was
the Englishman's name—shook him by the hand in amazement,
expressed himself in agreement with Kant's exalted ideas, begged
forgiveness for his impetuosity, accompanied him as far as his
rooms in the evening and gave him a cordial invitation to visit
him. Green's partner, Motherby, was an eye-witness of this
occurrence and stated that, during this discourse, Kant had
seemed to him and to all those present as if inspired by a divine
power and had completely won their hearts.'

Out of this acquaintance, which arose under such remarkable
circumstances, there developed a cordial friendship, which Kant
valued highly. It was founded on mutual respect, became ever
firmer and more intimate and lasted until Green's death, which
Kant never quite got over. Kant found in Green a man of unusual knowledge and acute intelligence; he later propounded all
the most important principles of his philosophy to him, in order
to obtain the judgment of an intelligence, unbiased by attachment to any system, upon them.

Like Kant, Green was a bachelor, a man of the most excellent
character, distinguished by strict integrity and real nobility of
mind, but full of capricious idiosyncrasies, whose days were
passed according to an invariable and eccentric routine. Kant's
friend, Hippel, the town councillor and police superintendent,
who was also a writer, caricatured this strange fellow in his
comedy, *The Man by the Clock or the Regular Man*, which was
praised by Lessing. The story is told of how Kant had, one evening, promised Green to go for a drive with him the following
morning at eight o'clock. Green, who on such occasions was
accustomed to pace up and down the room with his watch in
his hand at a quarter to, and to put his hat on at ten to, picked up
his stick at five to and, at the first stroke of the hour, opened

the carriage door and drove on. He met Kant, who was two minutes late, coming to meet him, but he did not stop because this was contrary to their arrangement and to his routine.

This singular, but noble-minded man had so much to offer the mind and heart of Kant that he became his daily companion, with whom he spent several hours every day. As Jachmann recounts, Kant used to go to Green's house almost every afternoon; there he used to 'find Green asleep in an easy chair, sit down beside him and, lost in meditation, fall asleep himself. Then Bank Director Ruffmann usually came in and followed suit, till finally, at a certain time, Motherby entered the room and woke the sleeping company, who then engaged in the most interesting conversation till seven o'clock. They used to part so punctually at seven that people living in the street were in the habit of saying it could not be seven o'clock yet, because Professor Kant had not gone past.'

Without intruding into his friends' private affairs, Kant gave them advice tactfully and with great delicacy of feeling and was happy when he could be of service to them. When opportunity arose, he did whatever he could to help them, without letting them know that he had been active on their behalf.

Anyone who had formed a picture of Kant on the basis of the critical philosopher's profound and abstract works and imagined him withdrawn and secluded, was always very much surprised, on meeting him personally, to find him excellent company. He combined, in the happiest manner, profound learning with fine social polish. He was no unworldly bookworm, but stood in the midst of life, which had been his school. No one could form a true picture of him from his writings and his lectures alone; only in society did the complete man of worldly wisdom become evident. How he appeared against this background we learn from one of his best friends, Jachmann, the most reliable of sources.

'Kant possessed the great art of conversing in an interesting manner on any topic in the world. His wide learning, which extended to the smallest affairs of everyday life, provided him with a wealth of conversational material, which his original mind, with its own way of looking at everything, invested with a new and characteristic form. There was no matter involved in human existence upon which Kant did not, on occasion, speak; but the most insignificant matter became of interest through the manner in which Kant dealt with it. He knew how to approach everything from the most noteworthy and instructive angle; he was skilled in throwing the qualities of a thing into relief by means of comparison; he knew how to state the manifold usefulness and the most indirect effects of even the least concern; in his hands the smallest thing became great, the most insignificant important. Hence, in society, he could converse with anyone, and his conversation awakened general interest. He discussed women's affairs with women as instructively as matters of science with scholars. In his company conversation never flagged. He had only to choose some subject at random from the wealth of his knowledge, to weave around it the threads of an entertaining conversation.

'In large gatherings, even of scholars, Kant avoided discussion of specifically academic subjects; least of all was he ever heard to engage in argumentation on the topics of his philosophy. I do not remember him ever having mentioned one of his own works in company, or having referred to their contents. In social conversation, even when the subject was some concern of science or philosophy, he was careful to draw easily apprehended inferences, which he then applied to everyday life. Just as he knew how to increase the importance of minor matters by the viewpoint he adopted in presenting them, so he possessed the capacity of bringing sublime reasoning down to the level of common understanding by applying it to everyday life. It is remarkable that the man, who expressed himself so obscurely while deriving philosophical proof from first principles, was capable of such clarity of expression in the application of philosophical conclusions. In society, the obscure critical sage became a lucid popular philosopher. He discarded academic language entirely, and clothed his thoughts in common speech. He did not follow the rules of academic demonstration, but allowed his discourse to wander at will, dealing now at length, now briefly with any subject which took his fancy, according to the extent to which

it held his interest and that of the company in which he found
himself.

'At table, particularly, his conversation was absolutely inex-
haustible. If the company's number was not much greater than
that of the Muses, so that *one* conversation governed the whole
table, *he* was generally the spokesman, not that he usurped this
role, but that everyone else very gladly left it to him. But, at
table, he was far from playing the Professor and delivering a
cohesive discourse; he merely directed the mutual exchanges of
the whole company. Objections and doubts imparted such
stimulus to his conversation that they were capable of arousing
him to the greatest vivacity. But he was as intolerant of stub-
born contradiction as of uncritical agreement. He liked lively,
quick-witted, talkative companions, whose intelligent remarks
and interjections gave him the occasion to develop his ideas and
present them in a satisfactory form.

'His social conversation was rendered particularly attractive by
the good humour with which he delivered it, the witty fancies
with which he adorned it and the appropriate anecdotes with
which he interspersed it. Good taste and gaiety prevailed in any
company where Kant was present. Everyone left it enriched in
knowledge and new ideas, content with himself and mankind,
fortified to fresh tasks and disposed to the benefaction of his
fellow-men. How much his social conversation meant to us for
both heart and head can be seen from the fact that many of his
hearers used to make a point of jotting down and elaborating on
his table-talk at home, just as they had formerly done with his
lectures. All his friends were unanimously of the opinion that
they had never known a more interesting companion.

'Kant was distinguished, however, not only by his conversational powers, but also by his social adroitness and tact. His de-
meanour combined a noble freedom and a lightheartedness
which was always in good taste. He was at ease in all kinds of
society, and his whole disposition showed that he had trained
himself in and for society. Speech and bearing gave evidence of
a fine sense of decorum and propriety. He possessed complete
social adaptability and was able to adopt the behaviour appro-

priate to any particular company in which he happened to be. He appeared as a well-bred man of the world, whose great inner worth was augmented by fine outward culture.' Thus Jachmann.

Since he was frequently invited to dine at the best homes of his native town, he took the greatest care over his outward appearance. When occasion offered he used to impress upon his hearers that, 'a man should never dress in a manner quite contrary to the fashion, it is an absolute duty to avoid presenting to anyone in the world an unpleasant or even an unnecessarily striking sight. He cited as a principle to be carefully followed that, amongst other things, the choice of the colours of coat and waistcoat should be made exactly according to the flowers. Nature produces nothing which is not pleasant to the eyes; the colours which she places alongside each other always harmonize with one another. Thus, for instance, a yellow waistcoat goes with a brown coat, as is proved by the auriculae. Later he had a particular liking for variegated colours. He always attached importance to well-chosen clothes.'

As to his physical constitution, it was hardly to be expected that he would be granted eighty years of life. He managed to wring his great age from nature by his prudence, his energy and his self-mastery. It seemed to his contemporaries that, in making the philosopher, nature had used the whole material for the mental part, giving him a mind of exceptional dimensions at the expense of his body. Kant was of small stature and his flat, almost concave chest and somewhat raised right shoulder gave him a slightly stooped appearance. He was hardly five feet in height and very delicately built, with a disproportionately large head. His most striking facial characteristics were his broad brow with bosses over the root of the nose, his thin, imposing nose and the unusually luminous blue eyes. The upper portion of the face was reminiscent of Frederick the Great, the lower, with its finely drawn lines, of Johann Caspar Lavater. He had a hypersensitive nervous system, 'a sheet of newsprint, fresh and damp from the press, was enough to give him catarrh' (Jachmann).

In spite of his feeble physique, Kant was never really ill during the whole of his life; though he was frequently indisposed, and often suffered from gastric disorder, the only malady of which he made frequent complaint and to combat which he took pills. He observed himself so closely that he immediately noticed any change in his body and was able to take counter-measures in good time. Kant often jested about his physical weakness; thus he one day remarked that the only reason he never wore black stockings was that they made the calves look thinner than they really were and his 'were quite thin enough already'. He also made merry over the fact that his old manservant never passed behind his table without placing his hair-bag, which always slipped over from the higher shoulder-blade to the lower, in the centre of his back, with the most serious mien, in order to render his deformity less noticeable.

9

Daily Routine

THE FACT that, in spite of his delicate constitution, Kant lived to such a great age may have been due, in no small measure, to his moderate and strictly regulated manner of life. In later life he lived by the clock, like his closest friend, the odd-fellow Green, and kept to an inviolate daily routine.

He rose at five every morning, summer or winter. Punctually at a quarter to five his manservant came up to his bed in the absolutely dark bedroom.[1] He gave vent to a loud cry: 'It is time!' and did not leave the room till his master was out of bed. It often happened that Kant was so sleepy still that he would

---

[1] Kant had the remarkable idea that there was no better way of exterminating unwelcome 'guests' in the bedroom than complete darkness; for this reason, every ray of light was permanently excluded from the single window by means of a 'black-out', firmly attached from within.

have liked to stay in bed a little longer, and therefore told his servant to let him go on resting. But the latter had such firm orders not to be misled by this, that he ruthlessly compelled him to get up punctually.

As soon as Kant was dressed, he went into his study, wearing a dressing-gown, with a night-cap on his head, on top of which he placed a three-cornered hat; he sat down at the tea-table and immediately took breakfast, which consisted of two cups of tea, followed by a pipe of tobacco, the only one he permitted himself in the course of a day. The tea was an extremely weak infusion; he would far rather have had coffee, of which he was very fond, and it cost him the greatest effort to refrain from drinking it, especially when he was tempted by the aroma in company. But he considered the oil of coffee to be injurious, and therefore avoided it entirely. After breakfast he sat in meditation. 'This is the happiest time of the day for me,' he once remarked to his visitors Abegg[1] and Pastor Sommer on 12th June 1798; 'I do not exert myself, but gradually gather my forces, and it is during this time that I eventually decide upon the day's tasks.' He spent the hour from six to seven preparing his lectures. He then dressed with care and made his way to the lecture-room, which was in his own house. At nine he returned to his study, where he worked concentratedly till a quarter to one.

After he had ceased to eat at an inn, this was the time when he received dinner-guests; he generally remained at table till about four o'clock. After this he went for an hour's walk, or longer if the weather were especially fine. He had to take care not to sit down in an arm-chair between eating and going out for a walk, because, had he done so, he could not have resisted falling asleep and he wished particularly to avoid sleeping after a meal.

His route usually led along the 'Philosophic Walk' or 'Philosophers' Embankment', upon which in the seventies, as he himself recounts, the leading ideas of his *Critique of Pure Reason* came into being, to the charmingly situated Friedrichsburg Castle on the left bank of the Pregel. Whereas, in his earlier years, he used

---

[1] Abegg, Johann Friedrich, a theologian from Baden, who kept a journal of his conversations with Kant.

Kant and his circle at table, a painting by Emil Doestling

Kant, a bust by Friedrich Hagemann, 1801

to invite an acquaintance or one of his students with whom he was personally friendly to accompany him, he later preferred to do without company, partly in order to pursue his thoughts undisturbed and partly because he considered it healthier to breathe through the nose than through the mouth, while walking. Because he was frequently followed by beggars and importunate acquaintances, he had to make occasional changes of route. He did not easily allow the weather to put a stop to his strolls. In summer he used to walk very slowly so as not to break into a sweat, which he believed he had to avoid on account of his constitution.

After returning from his walk he used to read. He looked through the periodicals and political papers which had been delivered to him and liked to read travel books and works on natural science. At dusk he liked to think over what he had read or jot down his passing thoughts in a memorandum. Punctually at ten he laid aside the affairs of the day and went to bed. In his later years, every day passed in this manner and nothing was allowed to break the routine.

During his last years, Kant only ate once a day, at midday, but then with a very hearty appetite. Throughout the whole of the rest of the day he took nothing but water. He would not touch beer, which he called a food, because beer contained so much nourishment that beer-drinkers satisfied their hunger with it and so spoilt their appetite for real food. At his midday meal he drank only some red wine, generally Médoc. A small quarter-bottle stood before him and before each of his guests, and usually no more than this small quantity was drunk.

Kant liked sleeping in a cold bedroom; he only had it warmed at times of severe cold, which were not unusual in his native town. This suited him and his sleep was deep and peaceful. The weather had a great influence on his well-being, which led him always to observe it carefully. As he became increasingly infirm, he spoke more frequently of his physical condition. There can hardly have been anyone who paid greater attention to the state of his health than Kant. He attached the greatest importance to living as long as possible and, as Jachmann mentions, for many years he had the Königsberg police authorities supply him with the monthly list of deaths, in order to calculate therefrom his probable expectation of life. But the weaker and more susceptible was his body, the stronger and more resistant was his mind, which dominated his body. It was his firm purpose, as he explained in a brief treatise,[1] to master his morbid feelings by means of earnest resolution.

10

Character and Personality

K ANT was not merely worthy of admiration for his mind and his comprehensive learning, he was not only a truly great and celebrated thinker and an academic teacher of distinction, but also a man of outstanding character. The natural inclinations of his heart disposed him to benevolence and philanthropy and these inclinations were confirmed by the ethical principles of his philosophy, the products of his reason. His life and his teaching were one. In his relations with his fellow-men he was guided, not by his emotions, but by ethical principles, by the ordinances of duty. His whole mode of living was consistently regulated by reason, which governed over his inclinations and impulses. Whatever he had once recognized as his duty, he put into execution strictly and without delay. An example of this: 'The bookseller, Nicolovius, whose father was a friend of Kant's, decided, while he was at the University, to devote himself to bookselling and communicated his decision to Kant. He approved of the plan and remarked in passing that he would do what he could to assist his establishment. Hardly had Nicolovius set up his bookshop in Königsberg, than Kant gave him

---

[1] *On the Power of the Mind to Master Morbid Feelings by Resolution Alone* (1798).

his works for publication for a very low fee per sheet. Shortly after, a German publishing house of standing approached the world-renowned author and offered him a vastly higher sum; but Kant replied that he himself found the fee excessive and that he regarded it as his patriotic duty to render this slight service to his fellow-countryman, the son of his old friend.'

'The unshakable determination with which he fulfilled his duty to others was equalled by the firmness with which he treated himself. He was able to forbid himself everything, to overcome everything; for he was absolute master of himself. But he was not a capricious master and, hence, at the same time a slave in bondage; on the contrary, he was a sensible ruler over his own mode of life, who prescribed himself regulations after due deliberation and adhered to them with astonishing self-control until such time as his reason bade him exchange them for others, more in keeping with his nature, which he in turn observed strictly. He subordinated both his body and his whole mode of life to these rules of reason and owed his health and his long life to the strength of his character. Not merely in theory, but also in practice, he was a true sage.' (Jachmann)

Kant gladly accorded to others the recognition they had earned, as in general he judged his fellow-men by their moral worth. Sycophancy and social timidity were unknown to him, he was protected from them by his consciousness of his own value; even when confronted by his social superiors he was always true to his own character, and fearlessly stood up for his convictions and principles. He was never willing to purchase honours at the price of truth. To him veracity was the highest virtue and deceitfulness one of the worst vices.

Kant was no fighter; he detested uproar and strife and contented himself with formulating his ideas within himself, refraining from taking up any position in relation to learned controversies. He repeatedly asserted that he would never say anything he did not think, but, on the other hand, would naturally not have the courage to say everything he thought.

In spite of all his knowledge of the world and his intellectual superiority, there was something childlike about him, and he was very candid in his personal relations. His exalted ethical attitude compelled the respect of his fellows. 'Self-determination!' was his watchword. To his mind, the value of life lay in what one did, not in what one enjoyed. If he later showed a certain tendency to solitariness, this sprang from the fact that he had outgrown his environment and therefore withdrew into himself.

He eschewed emotional thinking; to his mind, life ought to be lived according to principles established by reason and not governed by inclinations and passions: 'Intelligence is the highest power of the soul, and it is a sad thing when the lord and master follows in the wake of the rabble of the passions.'

Kant was cheerful by nature. Even when disturbed in the midst of serious work, he did not lose his good humour. The equilibrium of his spirits was rarely perturbed by any intense emotion. Of course, as he wrote to his friend, Marcus Herz, in Berlin (24th November 1776), in consequence of his flat and narrow chest, which left little play for heart and lungs, he had a natural disposition to hypochondria, which, in his early years, almost led him to feel tired of life. 'But the reflexion that the cause of this cardiac oppression might be purely mechanical and irreversible soon led to my taking no further notice of it and, while I felt an oppression in my breast, calm and contentment held sway in my head and were unfailingly communicated to others.' Thus, in spite of his physical debility and frequent indisposition, he exhibited a serenity which made those around him cheerful too. He also had a sense of humour. He enjoyed reading witty and satiric authors and thought it valuable to ridicule the follies of mankind, not excluding one's own. As the best 'endowments of the soul' he considered 'a sound intelligence, a light heart and a free, self-governing will'.

His favourite maxims, which sum up his conception of life, were:

I am human, nothing human is foreign to me. (Terence)

Hold fast and hold yourself in check! The aim of your endeavours is within you, do not seek it outside. (Persius)

Do not give way to misfortune, but confront it with all the greater courage. (Virgil)

II

Kant and Art

HAD KANT any feeling or taste for art? In view of his outspoken predisposition to purely abstract thought this was hardly to be expected. The art of poetry was closest to him. He had even tried his own hand at it once or twice, and those small examples of his attempts which came to the eyes of Jachmann the latter considered, 'rich in ideas and powerfully expressed'. Kant regarded rhyme as being second only to poetic content in its importance in the constitution of a fine poem. 'He did not admit the claim of any poem to the title, if it were not in rhyme—or at least metrical. Unrhymed poetry he called prose gone mad and could find no pleasure in it whatever.' (Jachmann) Moreover, in his fortieth year, while he was still a magister, Kant was offered the chair of poetry at Königsberg University. At any rate, on the 5th August 1764 a letter from the Ministry in Berlin was addressed to the East Prussian administration saying: 'A certain Königsberg magister, by name Immanuel Kant, has come to our notice through some of his writings, which evince a very profound learning.' And the question was then put, 'has the latter given evidence of possessing the capabilities required by the post of Lecturer, has he distinguished himself in the domains of German and Latin poetry and would he be disposed to accept such a post?' If Kant had taken this office it would have entailed the supervision of all poems composed for special academic occasions; furthermore, he would have had to represent the University as official poet at all academic ceremonies. Not feeling this to be his vocation, he rejected the offer without giving it very much consideration.

Apart from the eloquence with which he propounded neat

pieces of reasoning in his lectures and the great pleasure he found in reading ancient and more modern works of rhetoric, the arts meant little to him—least of all music, although he did occasionally go to concerts of great masters. Kant himself played no musical instrument and advised anyone, who wished to devote himself to science, against doing so, on the grounds that it might too easily divert him from serious study.[1]

'Next to poetry,' writes Kant, 'if we are considering the stimulation and stirring of the heart, I should place that other aural art, which is the closest to it, and can be so naturally combined with it, namely music. For, although its message consists solely of sensations devoid of concepts and, unlike poetry, it leaves nothing behind it upon which to ponder, it nevertheless exercises a more complex and, though only momentarily, a more fervent influence upon the emotions; but it is, of course, enjoyment rather than culture and, judged by reason, is of less value than any of the other fine arts.'

Consequently, because music is not capable, through its own medium, of expressing ideas, but only of arousing emotions, so that the listener is obliged to produce his own concomitant thoughts, Kant did not rate it particularly highly; he took greater pleasure in music when it was combined with poetry. 'Music', he asserted, 'is able to put a poet or a philosopher in such a frame of mind as to enable each one to seize upon and master those thoughts which accord with his particular preoccupation and interests; it thus not only facilitates thought, but also incites it.'

---

[1] We would point to the similar opinions on this subject held by another philosopher, John Locke (1632–1704), who wrote in his *Some Thoughts concerning Education*: 'If a child have a poetic vein, it is to me the strangest thing in the world, that the father should desire or suffer it to be cherished or improved. Methinks the parents should labour to have it stifled and suppressed as much as may be; and I know not what reason a father can have to wish his son a poet, who does not desire to have him bid defiance to all other callings and business. . . . Poetry and gaming, which usually go together, are alike in this too, that they seldom bring any advantage. . . .'

'(Music) wastes so much of a young man's time, to gain but a moderate skill in it. . . . Our short lives will not serve us for the attainment of all things; nor can our minds be always intent on something to be learned.' (John Locke: *Some Thoughts concerning Education*, Ward, Lock & Co., London, pp. 131 and 150.)

The manner in which Kant, on occasion, reacted to music is reported by E. A. Ch. Wasianski, Deacon at Königsberg, who was an almost daily visitor to the philosopher during his last years and stood by him loyally to the end of his days:

'During this summer, the music of the mounting of the guard provided him with more passing entertainment than usual. When they marched past his house, he left the middle door of his back room, in which he lived, open and listened to the music with attention and pleasure. The profound metaphysician might have been expected to take delight only in music characterized by pure harmony, bold transitions and naturally resolved dissonances, or in the productions of serious composers, such as Haydn. But this was not the case, as is shown by the following:

'In the year 1795 he paid me a visit in the company of his friend G. R. von Hippel, in order to hear my spinet. An adagio on the flageolette pedal, which resembles the harmonica in tone, offended his ear rather than left him indifferent; but at full volume, with the lid open, the instrument pleased him mightily, especially when it imitated a symphony with full orchestra.'

He could never recall without repugnance the occasion on which he had been present at a performance of funeral music on the death of Moses Mendelssohn, which had consisted, in his own expression, of a ceaseless, tedious whining. He presumed, he said, that other sentiments, such as triumph over death (calling for heroic music), or consummation should have also found expression. He came near to making a precipitate departure. After this cantata, he gave up attending concerts, for fear of suffering a similar martyrdom again.

12

Kant and His Brother and Sisters

K ANT'S ATTITUDE to his brother and sisters has not always been judged aright and has given rise to misinterpretations of his character.

His only brother, Johann Heinrich (born 1735), grew up in the household of their uncle Richter, whom we have mentioned earlier on, after the father's death. After studying theology in Königsberg, he was obliged to earn his living as a private tutor with various families in Courland. Only in 1774 did he become senior assistant master and, a year later, headmaster at Mitau municipal school. As the vocation of a minister later came to appeal to him more strongly, he took over the pastorate of the Courland village of Altrahden, where he enjoyed a happy family life with his wife, Marie Havemann, and their four children.

There was no close contact between the brothers. The celebrated Königsberg relation certainly received frequent letters from his younger brother, as well as from the latter's daughter, written in a cordial tone. But the great philosopher's replies were rare and coolly objective rather than cordial.

Thus Pastor Johann Heinrich Kant wrote to Königsberg on the 21st August 1789:

'After we have passed so many years without any exchange of letters, you will perhaps not think it inopportune that we should once more approach each other. We are both aged, how soon one of us will pass over into eternity. . . . Come, dearest brother, let me know, however briefly, what your state of health has been and now is and what further scholarly thoughts are germinating in your mind for the enlightenment of present and future generations. And do not forget to give me news of our surviving sisters. I will, with pleasure, pay the postage on your letter, even if it occupies no more than one side of an octavo sheet. . . .'[1]

Of course, it was some time before Kant answered his brother. On the 26th January 1792, that is some two and a half years later, he informed him that 'a mass of work' had prevented him from replying sooner.

'In spite of my apparent indifference, I am at length refreshing your memory of me with a letter. . . . Not only do I often think of you with brotherly feelings now, while we are both living, but you will also be sensible of my thought for you after my death, which, at the age of 68, can no longer be very distant. Two of our remaining sisters, both of them widowed, are being entirely cared for by myself, while the third, for whom a place in St. George's Hospital has been bought, receives an allowance from me. I have also not refused my aid to the children of the former in setting up house, so that I have not failed in the fulfilment of the debt of gratitude which I owe to our mutual parents for their upbringing. . . .'[2]

When Johann Heinrich died in February 1800, leaving his family in very modest circumstances, Kant came to their assistance with an annual allowance of two hundred Taler. His three nieces married during the lifetime of their uncle; in his will he left half his fortune, after deduction of legacies, i.e. some 20,000 Taler, to his brother's heirs.

Three of the philosopher's sisters (born 1727, 1730 and 1731) originally occupied humble domestic posts in Königsberg and then married simple craftsmen. One of them, Maria Elisabeth, was divorced by her husband, upon which her brother Immanuel came to her aid, on account of her distressed circumstances, and supported her till her death after a long illness in 1796; thereupon, he doubled her 'pension' and continued to pay it to her children and grandchildren, as is witnessed by the following letter from the philosopher to his brother, Johann Heinrich Kant:

[1] *Complete Works of Kant*, Academy Edition, vol. xi, p. 69.
[2] ibid, vol. xi, p. 307.

'Dear Brother, the changes which have taken place in our family here consist in the fact that death took away your eldest sister last summer after a long illness, so that the allowance I have been making her since 1768 fell vacant; but I doubled it and paid it to her surviving children. I am making a further allowance to our only other living sister, Barbara, who is otherwise well cared for in St. George's Hospital. I have, therefore, provided for all my sisters as well as for their numerous children, some of whom have children of their own. I shall continue to shield them from want until my own place in the world also falls vacant, and I hope that even then some not inconsiderable sum will remain for my relations and brothers and sisters.

'Königsberg, 17th December 1796.'[1]

The only sister to outlive Kant was the youngest, Barbara Theuer, whom he had taken care of in St. George's Hospital (as stated in his letter). She had been a widow for many years, her husband having died during the first year of their marriage. In his last year of life, Kant took her into his household, where she loyally helped tend him till his death. She was only six years younger than her brother, but still rather lively and gay. Kant, who, in his last years, disliked having anyone around him, quickly grew accustomed to her. He valued her greatly for her modesty and discretion and her trustworthy care of him. She possessed the patience and forbearance demanded, in caring for him, by his advancing weakness. She died a few years after her brother, on the 28th January 1807.

It will certainly have struck the reader that for many years Kant was precious little concerned about his brother and sisters, although he lived in the same town, and had absolutely no contact with them. But this was certainly not the outcome of pride; in the first place, it was due to the fact that he had so far outgrown their orbit as to have very little in common with them.

And if his relations with his cultured brother, Johann Heinrich, the Courland pastor, were not very active either, this was because, by the standards of those days, the latter lived at too

[1] ibid, vol. xii, p. 139.

great a distance. Moreover, Kant was not an assiduous letter-writer; not more than about three hundred letters written by him have come to light—very few in relation to the length of his life. He frequently apologized for his 'negligence' and 'apathy' in writing.

But he faithfully followed towards his brother and sisters his ethical principles, which bade him value duty and obligation higher than mere goodwill and love.

13

Kant in Old Age

WHEREAS IN HIS earlier years Kant usually took his meals in an inn, from his sixty-third year onward he ran his own household. As already mentioned, he came into possession, in 1783, of a somewhat old-fashioned house in the neighbourhood of the Castle. He had eight rooms on two stories. One side of the ground floor was occupied by Kant's lecture-room, the other by his old cook's rooms; on the upper floor were situated his dining-room and bedroom, in which he had placed his not very extensive library, together with his reception room and study, which faced east and enjoyed an uninterrupted outlook over some gardens. His old manservant, Lampe, lived in a small attic.

One of his later dinner companions, his colleague, Johann Gottfried Hasse, has drawn us a vivid picture of the impression offered by Kant's house to a visitor.[1]

'Everything about the house announced its owner to be a philosopher. It stood in an accessible but not much frequented

[1] Hasse, J. G.: *Notable Utterances of Kant.* By one of his table companions. Königsberg, 1804. Republished by Arthur Buchenau and Gertrud Lehmann (*Kant in Old Age*), Berlin, 1925.

street and backed on to gardens and the moat, beyond which lay the rear buildings of the many hundred years old Castle, with its towers, dungeons and owls. In spring and summer the district was truly romantic; not that he actually enjoyed it—he merely saw it.

'On entering the house, a peaceful silence reigned such that, if the open kitchen smelling of food, a barking dog or a miaowing cat, darlings of his cook (who, as Kant said, carried on whole discourses with them) had not proved the contrary, it might have been thought uninhabited. At the top of the stairs, the servants were to be seen laying the table in the room on the right. An ante-room led, through a plain, almost shabby door, into the humble "Sans-Souci"; a knock on the door would be answered by a cheerful "Come in!". The whole room breathed simplicity and seclusion from the clamour of the town and the world. Two ordinary tables, a simple sofa and a few chairs, amongst them a reading-chair, and a chest of drawers topped by an undistinguished looking mirror left a space in the centre of the room, enabling him to approach the barometer and thermometer, which he consulted assiduously. The costliest items in the room were probably the little green silk curtains on the small-paned windows.

'Here sat the thinker on his all-wood, semicircular chair, or else upon a three-legged stool, either still at his desk or already turned towards the door, because he was hungry and eagerly awaiting his guests. He rose to meet the latter, opened the door slightly and gave them a hearty welcome.'

Because Kant did not like dining alone, to which his earlier habits had made him unaccustomed, he regularly invited one or two table companions, which, on special occasions, was usually increased to five or six. Kant was of the opinion that if each one of a company at table was to have something of the others, the company must be small. The number of guests should not be less than the number of the Graces (three), nor greater than that of the Muses (nine). His midday dinner-parties were celebrated throughout Königsberg.

He did not invite his guests, who were always different, until the morning of the same day, because he then felt certain that they would not receive any subsequent invitation; for he did not want anyone to have to refuse another offer on his account. As a host, Kant combined a courteous attentiveness with his social refinement; he did all he could to entertain his guests in the most pleasant manner, he even took note of their favourite dishes and had these served to them. Guests felt so unconstrained at Kant's table that they expressed their wishes freely, feeling absolutely at home.

The midday meal offered Kant a welcome opportunity for intellectual diversion. For this reason, it not infrequently lasted till four in the afternoon, or even longer. 'Usually', as Jachmann informs us, 'he had put by letters or other items of news which he communicated to his friends either before or at table, and to which he linked further conversation. Conversation at his table was similar, on the whole, to that at other such gatherings, apart from the fact that it was more frank and intimate. Here words came more from the heart, here the great man discussed his own and his friends' affairs, here the philosopher could be seen with constraint cast aside, relaxing from his strenuous mental labours, here he freely pursued every idea which came to his mind and gave rein to every feeling which sprang from his heart, here Kant appeared in his own natural guise. And how indescribably lovable he did appear on these occasions! Only by seeing him here and directly experiencing his rare qualities and way of dealing with people, could his greatness be fully appreciated. The bright light of wisdom and the generous warmth of a sympathetic heart, earnest concern for the sufferings of humanity and exhilarating joy at the beautiful and gladdening things of the world here alternated and intermingled in the most delightful manner and gave spice to the philosopher's simple table.'

The twenty-three-year-old mining student from Memmingen, Friedrich Lupin, visited Kant with letters of recommendation from Göttingen scholars in 1794, and was invited to dine with him on the following day. He has left us an account of his impressions and experiences at this meal.

Whereas, on the previous day, he had seen the philosopher in his dressing-gown, on this occasion the latter received him fastidiously dressed, in the fashion of a hospitable master of the house, with a pride of manner which came from within and was admirably suited to him. 'He seemed different, less dry in body and soul than the man of yesterday in the dressing-gown, even though the suit gave him a more emaciated appearance. But his high, serene brow and clear eyes were the same and crowned and animated the little man, above whom I towered like a shadow above the person who throws it. Kant attacked the food and the good, old wine with such relish (in his latter years he only ate once a day and therefore had a long fast behind him when he sat down to table), that he spoke little during the meal. Immediately afterwards, however, he became very communicative. I have seen few men of his age as lively and sprightly as he. The remarks which he himself passed on even the most unimportant matters, were made in a manner as dry as their content was witty and pointed. He interspersed his conversation with anecdotes so appropriate that they seemed made to order for that particular moment; his listeners, who were just expecting the most serious point to be made, could not restrain their laughter.

That his profound thought was in no way detrimental to cheerful sociability was the great man's foremost trait; he was compounded of pure reason and profound intelligence, but not, on this account, a burden either to himself or to others. To be happy in his company one had only to watch him and listen to him, to be virtuous not merely to believe his words, but only to follow his example and think as he did; for there can hardly have been a more moral life than his. . . .'[1]

Kant's aged manservant, the Würzburg-born Martin Lampe, played a special role in his household. He had seen long service as a soldier in the Prussian army, and had been in Kant's employ since the early sixties. Since his master had come into possession of his own house his self-esteem had been greatly augmented; he thought himself 'butler, steward, and bailiff' and the superior of the old cook, which frequently led to disagreeable quarrels. He was slightly weak-minded, being unable either to read or

[1] *Lupin's Visit to Kant.* 'Altpreussische Monatshefte', 38, nos. 7 and 8.

write, as Kant himself remarked in one of his notebooks; but he used to pick up utterances overheard in discussions at table and often repeated them in a distorted form, frequently with highly comical effect. Initially Lampe behaved well; his master valued him for his loyalty and trustworthiness and confidently entrusted him with the whole running of the household. But Lampe soon took very mean advantage of his master's benevolence, continually demanding extra pay, coming home excessively late at night, quarrelling with the maidservant and becoming increasingly useless.

When Kant engaged a new cook in 1793, the latter made it a primary condition of her acceptance of the position that she should herself be responsible for 'everything to do with the cooking', not wishing to be in any way dependent upon Lampe. The servant's unseemly behaviour led to increasing tension with Kant, who repeatedly thought of discharging him. He once made a note to the effect: 'Ask Police Superintendent Jensch how to get rid of my drunken servant Lampe.' To maintain order in the house, Kant had finally to see to every trifle himself.

Of this factotum who went down to history, Vorländer[1] recounts: 'The servant wore a livery of a white coat with a red collar. His master seems to have taken precious little interest in the life of the servant who had been with him for many years—forty altogether. Thus he first learnt that Lampe was about to enter, for the second time, into the holy state of matrimony on the following day, when the latter suddenly got himself a yellow coat in addition to his livery. He had apparently been previously married for many years, without his master's knowledge.

'One morning Lampe said to Kant: "Professor! They won't let me." To which Kant rejoined: "Who won't let you, or what won't they let you?"—"Oh, they won't marry me, because it's Lent."—"Well, I'll write to the Minister!"—"No, that's no use, one has to apply to the Bishop! When I married for the first time sixteen years ago, I had to make an application to the Bishop as well."—"So, he's been married once already, and he's a catholic!" '

[1] Vorländer II, p. 8 f.

In his latter years, Lampe became increasingly burdensome to Kant, partly because, while the servant's strength visibly declined, the now very frail philosopher had an ever greater need of a younger and more robust man. Lampe's discharge, which Kant had for long refused to consider, because he had repeatedly credited his servant's vows of reform, was finally accomplished in January 1802. Kant remarked to Wasianski,[1] who looked after him during his latter years, visiting him daily, that Lampe had once more behaved towards him so badly that he was ashamed to speak of it. Wasianski had foreseen and provided for this situation; he fetched the servant who was already waiting to take Lampe's place, one Johann Kaufmann, and on the following day Lampe was dismissed. In his generosity, Kant had arranged for him to receive a pension for life of forty Taler, with the proviso that it should cease immediately if Lampe, or anyone acting on his behalf, should importune him. Lampe demanded a reference for his services. 'For a long time', reports Waisianski, 'Kant could not make up his mind how to fill in the space left blank for "behaviour". Eventually he wrote: "He behaved conscientiously, but in a manner no longer in keeping with my requirements."'

The new servant, known as Johannes, proved very suitable and quickly developed a real love and attachment to his master. Peace and order once more ruled in the house, which Kant found very beneficial. Everything followed its regular pattern again; for Kant, in his old age, having become accustomed to a pedantically exact routine of life, was intolerant of the slightest alteration or disturbance of his habits.

---

[1] Wasianski, E. A. Ch., Deacon in Königsberg. *Immanuel Kant during the last years of his life. A Contribution to the Understanding of his Character and domestic life from daily association with him.* Königsberg, 1804.

Kant's tomb at Königsberg Cathedral

Critik
der
reinen Vernunft

von

Immanuel Kant
Profeſſor in Königsberg.

Riga,
verlegts Johann Friedrich Hartknoch
1781.

Title-page from Kant's "Critique of Pure Reason"

14

Kant's Conflict with Prussian Reaction

POLITICAL CHANGES in Prussia, including the particularly
unfavourable political situation in the eighties, brought
Kant into a remarkable conflict with the Administration
towards the end of his academic career.

Frederick the Great, the king of the Enlightenment, a friend of
tolerance, who had secured for his subjects freedom of creed and
conscience for all Christian denominations, died on the 17th
August 1786. He was succeeded by his nephew, Frederick
William II, who, during the first years of his reign, was well disposed towards Kant and gave repeated proof of his especial
esteem for him. But he showed less inclination for science than
for mystical and supernatural matters, which, at that time, were
the active concern of visionary and fantastic spirits—particularly
in polite society. This thirst for the supernatural was exploited
by swindlers like Cagliostro, who succeeded in amassing for-
tunes by their magical flummeries. Rosicrucians[1] and necro-
mancers were the fashion and were winning converts to their
church in Catholic and Protestant countries.

Even as Crown Prince, Frederick William II had been friendly
with the orthodox theologian Johann Christoph Wöllner and,
under his influence and through his interest in the miraculous,
had himself joined the Rosicrucian Order. As early as 1781 Kant
was informed by a friend that the members of this secret society
were working against the Enlightenment, which they claimed
to be 'atheistic' and the 'work of the devil'. At the appropriate
moment, i.e. on the death of Frederick the Great, they intended

[1] A secret order which came into being in the mid-eighteenth century, and
claimed possession of exceptional knowledge in the domains of theosophy,
magic and alchemy.

to enlist the throne in their struggle against the Frederician Enlightenment, and to re-establish the dominion of biblical and ecclesiastical belief in miracles, of pure and unadulterated religion. As his tool for this purpose the new king had destined the theologian Wöllner, whom Frederick the Great had once characterized in one of his famous marginal notes as 'a treacherous and intriguing priest, nothing more'.

Shortly after Frederick's death, the attack on the exponents of enlightenment was opened by the dismissal of his Ministers, above all Zedlitz, Kant's upright admirer and benefactor. The latter was replaced, on the 3rd July 1788, by the aforementioned Johann Christian Wöllner, who was appointed Minister of State and Justice and placed at the head of the department of ecclesiastical affairs 'on grounds of special trust'. His first act, six days after his appointment, was to issue an edict on religion stating that even teachers of the Lutheran and Calvinist faiths were attempting to undermine the fundamental truths of holy scripture and shamelessly propagating innumerable errors under the false pretence of enlightenment. True, this edict promised the continued maintenance of tolerance and freedom of conscience, 'so long as each man peacefully fulfils his duties as a good citizen of the State, but keeps his own particular opinion to himself and carefully avoids diffusing it further or endeavouring to confuse and undermine the faith of others by persuasion'.

Then, on the 19th December 1788, there appeared a new Censorship Edict, aimed at setting the necessary bounds to 'the licence of the so-called enlighteners and the liberty of the Press, which was degenerating into offensiveness of the Press'. It stated that everything published within the country (of Prussia) or brought in from outside was to be subjected to strict supervision, and indicated that it was the royal will that the Censor should take measures against all publications opposed to the general principles of religion, to the State and to the existing social order.

But the cause of reaction was also furthered by historical events. France, following the Revolution, was plunging ever more rapidly into unbridled licence. Sympathy with this political movement, which was evidenced in certain quarters, appeared to threaten Germany's internal security. In consequence of the Jacobin rule of terror, every libertarian demand was denounced as 'Jacobism'. Enemy of the Church, enemy of the State and supporter of the 'French freedom fraud' were taken as one and the same thing and soon became a general accusation against all free thinkers. Thus the leaders of reaction in Prussia looked upon all those who, like Kant, sympathized with the French Revolution, as 'revolutionaries' and, consequently, as 'extremely dangerous and evil-disposed persons'. A fresh edict dated 5th March 1792 intensified the censorship, so that now 'all disrespectful criticism of the laws of the land or of the internal administration were to be severely punished'. The King himself called for harsher measures against the 'subversive enlighteners and scoffers at religion'.

The publication of Kant's writings on political and religious subjects took place in this tense and troubled period, including his book, *Religion within the Limits of Reason Alone* (1793), which aroused such interest that a second edition was required the following year. This will be dealt with later in connection with Kant's philosophy.

Although Kant's unconcern had led to warnings from various quarters, a year later (June 1794) he published in a monthly periodical an essay on *The End of all Things*, in the concluding section of which he made no secret of his opposition to the reactionary trend of the times. For he observed: Instead of leaving things as they have been for nearly a generation, during which time they have given proof of reasonably good results, men 'of great, or at least, enterprising spirit'—as he ironically designates them—are now seeking other means of purifying and stimulating religion in a whole nation; the means consisting in the use of authority and commandment operating with promises of reward and threats of punishment. But such methods eat away the very core of Christianity, namely its loving-kindness, and if continued they will lead—in biblical terms—to the rule of 'Anti-Christ', founded on fear and self-interest, though this rule will not last for long.

Steps were now considered against Kant as well. He was well

aware, through his friends, of the position at the Berlin Court, of how the ecclesiastical dignitaries tyrannized over the King who, weak in body and soul, 'sits for hours weeping and has several times seen visions of Our Lord, Jesus'. In March 1794, the King himself had already written to Wöllner: 'The time has come to put a stop to Kant's noxious writings.'

On the 1st October, the following royal order-in-cabinet, drawn up by Wöllner, was addressed to 'Our venerable and learned Professor, as well as beloved and loyal Kant':

'For some considerable time Our Most Exalted Person has observed with great displeasure how you have misused your philosophy to the misrepresentation and depreciation of many of the principal and fundamental teachings of Holy Writ and of the Christian Religion, to whit in your book, *Religion within the Limits of Reason Alone*, as well as in other short treatises. We expected better of you, since you yourself must be conscious of your lack of responsibility both towards your duty as a teacher of youth and our sovereign intentions, of which you are fully aware. We immediately demand of you the conscientious acceptance of your responsibilities and we expect you, on pain of our highest displeasure, not to allow yourself to be guilty of any future acts of this nature, but rather, in accordance with your duty, to devote your authority and your talents to the ever increasing achievement of our sovereign purposes; if, on the contrary, you persist in your rebellion, you will not fail to suffer disagreeable consequences.

'You enjoy our favour.'

Kant replied at length that as a 'teacher of youth', i.e. in his lectures, he had not even touched upon either the Bible or the Christian religion. The book on religion referred to was beyond the comprehension of the general public and only intended for scholars of the faculty, who must possess the right of free enquiry, whereas the teachers of the people, in churches and schools, were naturally bound to the 'official religion of the country'. Nor did the book contain any evaluation of Christianity, but only of natural religion. Christianity's highest commendation consisted in its harmony with the purest moral tenets of reason, as was pointed out in his book. He made this reply with the absolutely sincere conscientiousness of a man in the seventy-first year of his age, who might soon have to answer to a judge of the universe.

In consequence of his deeply-rooted conviction of the duty of a subject, Kant decided, without hesitation or prolonged inward conflict, upon a solemn declaration that in future, 'as Your Royal Majesty's most loyal subject', he would 'refrain absolutely from all public pronouncements on the subject of religion, whether natural or revealed, in either lectures or written works'. In connection with this affair, the following words were found on a sheet of notepaper amongst his posthumous effects: 'Recantation and denial of an inner conviction is despicable; but in a case like the present it is the duty of a subject to remain silent; and, while one should never speak anything but the truth, it is not, therefore, one's duty to speak the whole truth in public.'

Following the death of Frederick William II, which took place soon after this (10th November 1797), Kant no longer felt bound by the promise which, 'as Your Royal Majesty's most loyal subject', he had given to this particular king only.

Kant had been greatly affected by this attack upon his teaching and literary activities; he had grown tired and at the end of the summer session, 1796, at the age of seventy-two, he gave up lecturing 'on the grounds of old age and indisposition'.

Kant's retirement from his academic post was made the occasion of a solemn farewell by his students, who, on the 14th June 1797, marched in a column to his house, accompanied by several bands of musicians, and there presented him with a poem written in his honour, celebrating him as one of the greatest scholars of all time. The last stanza ran:

> More than *eighteen thousand* days have gone
> Since first your fame as a teacher shone,
> Still, as in youth, your spirit just the same
> Up to the highest peaks of truth takes flight,
> Into the deepest obscurity casts light,
> Despite the trembling weakness of its frame.

15

Life's End

K ANT'S FRIEND, E. A. Ch. Wasianski, who, as has already
been mentioned, used to visit him almost every day during the last years of his life, in order to assist him with
domestic matters, has left us an extraordinarily detailed and faithful picture of Kant at this period.

The disintegration of his physical and mental powers took
place quite gradually. The first signs of disturbed health had already made their appearance in the early nineties; Kant describes
them as follows in a letter, dated 21st September 1791, to his
former listener, K. L. Reinhold:[1]

'. . . Some two years ago, without visible cause or actual illness, my health underwent a sudden revolution, which rapidly
upset my appetite for my habitual everyday pleasures, leaving
my physical powers and sensibilities unaffected, but greatly re-
ducing my disposition to brainwork, even to the reading of my
lectures. I can only apply myself continuously to the former for
two or three hours every morning, after which it is interrupted
by drowsiness (in spite of an excellent night's sleep), which
necessitates my working at intervals only, with the result that
the work makes poor progress and I have to wait for the right
mood and then take advantage of it. It is, I believe, nothing more
nor less than old age, which brings everyone to a stop sooner
or later, but is all the more unwelcome to me because I feel that
I am nearing the completion of my plan.'[2]

Nevertheless, Kant managed to carry on with his activities as

---

[1] Reinhold, Karl Leonhard (1758–1823), philosopher in Kiel. Made a valuable
contribution to the understanding of critical philosophy through his *Letters on
Kantian Philosophy* (1786).
[2] *Complete Works of Kant*, Academy Edition, vol. xi, p. 275.

teacher and writer for a few more years. But towards the end of the nineties a striking decline in his formerly excellent memory became evident, which made it necessary for him to write down everything he wished to bear in mind on so-called memoranda. However, he still hoped to be able to conclude his 'critical business' and fill the remaining gap with his paper: *Transition from the Metaphysical Foundations of Natural Science to Physics*. He worked assiduously at this book right into 1801, but only some portions of it appeared posthumously.

Marasmus laid ever tighter hold upon him; it was no specific disease of old age from which he suffered, but a gradual mental and physical devitalization. He suffered from frightful dreams, in which he felt himself to be surrounded by robbers and murderers. It took him considerable time to calm down after awakening. His memory grew weaker and weaker, his muscles slackened, his gait became uncertain, he was hardly able to keep upright without support and complained of cardial flatulence and of constant pressure in his head, which some peculiar crotchet led him to attribute to the action of atmospheric electricity.

On the 22nd April 1803 he celebrated his seventy-ninth and last birthday, surrounded by all his table-friends. He had particularly looked forward to this day, but did not enjoy it as he had expected, because the numerous company, to which he was no longer accustomed, quickly tired him. In the autumn of the last year of his life, the vision of his right eye diminished—he had completely lost the sight of the left some years previously. He was now unable either to read or write, and Wasianski was obliged to take charge of all his affairs. He did not wish to receive visits any more; but if anyone insisted on seeing him, he would come out of his study into the front room for an instant and say: 'What do you see in a decrepit old man like me?'

On the 8th October 1803 he fell seriously ill for the first time in his life; it was probably a stroke. He was bedridden for some days, but recovered from his deep faint. He now took every medicine without resistance, which he had never done before. 'I don't mind dying,' he said, 'but don't kill me with medicine; when I am really ill and weak you can do what you like with

me; then I will put up with anything—but I won't take any pre-
servatives.'

At eleven o'clock on the 12th February 1804, Kant drew his
last breath. 'His death was a cessation of life, not a violent act of
nature,' reports Wasianski.

16

The Funeral

THE NEWS of Kant's death, which spread through the city
like wildfire, made a deep impression in many different
spheres. A Königsberg paper of the 12th February carried
the following announcement on its front page:

'This morning at eleven o'clock Immanuel Kant died here in
his eightieth year, of total inanition. The world knows and
honours his services towards the revision of speculative philosophy. As to the other things for which he was distinguished,
loyalty, benevolence, uprightness, sociability—the loss of these
will only be felt to the full in our own town, where also the
memory of the deceased will be preserved longest and with the
greatest honour.'

During the following days there was a ceremonial pilgrimage
to the little house of death, since many people wanted to see the
famous philosopher once more and no one was refused admit-
tance. His mortal remains were placed on a bier in the spacious
dining-room. His head rested on the cushion upon which his
students had once delivered their poem. His features had suffered
no noticeable change, but his body was completely emaciated. A
plaster cast was made of his head.

The dryness of the corpse enabled it to remain above ground
for a full sixteen days. The burial ceremony did not take place
until the 28th February. A vast mass of people waited in silence

Kant, an engraving by Raab, after a painting by Döbler 1791

Kant, a miniature by Fr. W. Senewaldt, 1786

in the streets. To the sound of all the bells of the city and the accompaniment of funeral music, the procession, in which students bore the coffin, wended its way to the University- or Cathedral-church, where it was received by the academic senate and conducted into the church, which had been decorated in a dignified manner. After a solemn memorial service, the body was interred in the Professors' Vault.

On Kant's eightieth birthday special funeral celebrations were held in the University and the occasion was taken to erect a bust of Kant, carved during his lifetime by the sculptor, Hagemann, in Carrara marble. Since the Professors' Vault ceased to serve as a burial place for members of the University a few years after Kant's death, it was transformed into a gallery for professors and students and named the 'Stoa Kantiana', in honour of Kant.

To-day Kant's bones rest in a portico borne by tall sandstone pillars, within which is a plain sarcophagus. This resting place was consecrated on the two hundredth anniversary of Kant's birth, on the 22nd April 1924.

A great commemoration was held on the hundredth anniversary of Kant's death, the 12th February 1904. On this occasion a bronze tablet was affixed to the wall of the Castle, bearing the imperishable words from the conclusion of his *Critique of Practical Reason*: 'Two things fill the heart with ever renewed and increasing wonderment and reverence, the more often and the more lastingly we meditate upon them:

The starry firmament above me
and the moral law within me.'

KANT'S PHILOSOPHY

Philosophy as a Science

PHILOSOPHY SEEKS to co-ordinate the general results of thought and of the individual sciences into a unified view of the world and of life, and to examine the presuppositions of all sciences, in so far as these lie within man himself. Such investigations have been carried out since time immemorial and are always being undertaken afresh. For this reason it was not so much Kant's intention to teach his hearers philosophy, as how to *philosophize*, i.e. the procedure and methods which must be employed in order to arrive at a unified *view of the world and of life*. But it is a toilsome and difficult path which leads to the apprehension of such ultimate associations of facts; many embark upon it, but far from all of them pursue it to the end. Their strength soon fails and soon their patience and their persistence.

'Philosophy is a high Alpine track', wrote Schopenhauer on the 8th September 1811 during his journey across the Harz mountains, 'its only approach is a steep path over sharp stones and piercing thorns: It is lonely, and the higher one goes the more barren it becomes; whoever follows it must know no dread, but leave everything behind him and confidently blaze his own trail through the cold snow. Time and again he will suddenly find himself on the brink of an abyss, looking down upon the green valley below: vertigo will seize him and drag him down towards it; but he must hold himself back, even if he has to stick the soles of his feet to the rocks with his own blood. In return he will soon see the world beneath him, its deserts and morasses will vanish, its unevennesses will be smoothed out, its discordant sounds will not reach him, its curved outline will be

---

[1] *Philo*, Greek friend; *sophia*, wisdom. Philosopher: friend of wisdom, philosophy: love of wisdom.

revealed. He himself will stand continually in pure, cool Alpine air and will see the sun while black night still lies below. . . .'

Philosophy deals, above all, with three major problems: Truth, Goodness and Beauty.

Truth: Does true cognition exist? How is true, correct and universally valid cognition achieved? Where do its boundaries lie?

Goodness: What are the principles governing good, ethically right conduct? What are the guiding lines for human conduct, and by what criteria is ethical volition to be valued?

Beauty: Are there laws of aesthetic disposition and conditions which objects of nature and art must satisfy in order to be beautiful, i.e. aesthetically valuable? What is the nature of the beautiful, the aesthetic?

Kant made a detailed analysis of all these problems in his major works, founded a new philosophy and gained himself a lasting reputation in the scientific world.

Kant's creative activity is contained in his '*critical works*', and these are the source of his influence, which extends into the present:

1781   Critique of Pure Reason[1] (theory of cognition).
1783   Prolegomena[2] to Any Future Metaphysics.
1785   Fundamental Principles of the Metaphysic of Morals.
1788   Critique of Practical Reason (ethics).
1790   Critique of Judgment (aesthetics).
1793   Religion within the Limits of Reason Alone (religious
            philosophy).
1795   Perpetual Peace; a Philosophical Project.
1797   Metaphysical First Principles of Jurisprudence.
            Metaphysical First Principles of Moral Philosophy.

[1] New edition, 1787.
[2] Prolegomena: preamble, introduction. A simplified and easily understood exposition of the leading ideas of *Critique of Pure Reason*. By 'reason' Kant understands the 'faculty of cognition'.

2

Kant's Theory of Cognition

WHILE HIS INTELLECTUAL development was still proceeding Kant was, naturally, dependent upon existing philosophical systems. Not that they dominated
him completely, but they exercised a strong influence over
him. From 1740 to 1760 he was absorbed in the views of
Leibniz and Wolff, the generally accepted doctrine at the time,
with which he combined Newton's natural philosophy; from
1760 to 1770 he took his line from the thought of the English
philosophers, above all of Locke and Hume, though he passed
beyond their empirical philosophy when he perceived its weak-
nesses. But the numerous short papers which he published up to
1770 are deeply imbued with the spirit of the Enlightenment, the
current philosophical trend.

At that time there were two conflicting views as to the origin
of our knowledge and our cognition.

All knowledge, all cognition, the English philosopher, John
Locke (1632–1704), taught in his book, *An Essay concerning
Human Understanding* (1690), springs from experience, that is
from without. There are no innate ideas or notions. The understanding contains nothing which has not previously been in the
senses. The stimuli of the external world, by their effect upon the
senses, impart impressions to the mind, initially a *tabula rasa*,
virgin paper, which develop upon it as upon a photographic
plate. In this process we play no active part, we merely absorb,
the external world mirrors itself in our minds.

According to Locke, this outer experience (sensation) is

[1] Translator's note: Cognition (Ger. *Erkenntnis*), act or faculty of knowing or
a piece of knowledge (Latin, *cognoscere*, to know).

paralleled by an inner one, obtained through the inward sense (reflection). The understanding works over these impressions acquired through the senses, compares, differentiates, combines. According to this conception, the world really is as it appears to us through our senses or our experience. This philosophical direction, representing the thesis that all our cognition proceeds from the functioning of our senses and, hence, from experience, is called *Sensationalism* or *Empiricism*. John Locke is the father of Empiricism.[1]

According to another conception, equally prevalent at the time, all cognition was supposed to spring from the human mind itself, from the *ratio* or reason (Descartes or Cartesius, 1650). Rationalism took the view that it was possible to evolve all truths from pure thought, independently of experience. This implied that the external world was a projection of the internal world and, hence, a mere 'appearance'.

This antithesis in the domain of cognition had led philosophy into a blind alley; there seemed no way out, since neither the empirical nor the rational solution appeared satisfactory.

Kant devoted ten years of the most profound thought to the problem of cognition. His decisive work on the subject, the *Critique of Pure Reason*, which he published in 1781 (second, revised edition 1787), matured in silence. Kant cut the Gordian knot by recognition of the fact that both conceptions held an element of truth, that our cognition springs *both* from experience *and* from pure thought. His philosophy has, for this reason, also been called the philosophy of *Both-And*. His *Critique* (art of differentiation, from the Greek *krinein*, to differentiate) aims at establishing what portion of the entirely artificial fabric of science derives from outer experience and what from the understanding.

This major work of Kant's, the *Critique of Pure Reason* is, of course, written in a language so difficult to follow, so abstract

---

[1] Sensationalism: derivation of all cognition from sense-perception and of all ideas from sensory experience. Empiricism: the standpoint that all knowledge is the outcome of reality-testing and that this is the sole well-spring of concepts (Greek *en*, in; *peirao*, try).

and devoid of all illustrative examples, that the majority of his contemporaries failed to understand it, which Kant found incomprehensible. He therefore took the pains, two years later, to write a somewhat more readily intelligible and shortened version, which was published in 1783 under the title *Prolegomena to Any Future Metaphysics*,[1] *claiming to be a Science*. This book forms the best introduction to Kant's philosophy.

What parts do experience and understanding (which Kant calls 'reason') play in our cognitions? What, in fact, are cognitions?

Cognition, says Kant, is a judgment, but one which is certain, that is, beyond all doubt, in other words a *necessary* judgment. All cognition is expressed in the form of judgments, i.e. in the assertion of something concerning an object, e.g. the water is tepid, the stone is heavy, the room is warm, dark, etc. These are judgments. Verbally, judgments are contained in predications. But all the above judgments are the products of experience and, consequently, neither necessary nor universal; they are only subjective. When someone says: It is warm in this room, he ought rather to say: It seems to me warm in this room; someone else might find it cool. On warm, cold, light, dark, heavy, light, sour, bitter, large, small, opinions differ. Here every judgment is subjective, i.e. based on personal feeling. Such judgments are, therefore, neither universal nor necessary, but contingent (accidental); for it is not always the case that the room is warm, or dark.

Necessary, universal judgments, i.e. judgments recognized as true or correct by everyone at all times, exist in physics and mathematics and, above all, in geometry. The statement that the sum of the angles in a triangle are equal to two right angles or 180 degrees, or that the external angle of a triangle is equal to the sum of the two interior opposite angles is recognized as correct without reference to experience, universally and 'from the first' (*a priori*). The validity of such statements for all innumer-

---

[1] Metaphysics, here in the Kantian sense: cognitions resulting from the exercise of pure reason, of the intelligence, i.e. cognition which lies outside experience.

able individual cases can be proved by a *single* example and does not require to be tested by experience. We know for certain, in advance, that these propositions possess universal validity.

How does this come about? The figures, with which geometry deals, are creations, ideal constructions of our own faculty of intuition,[1] of our mind; in each individual case, we only extract from the construction what we ourselves have previously placed into it. Every proposition in geometry depends for its validity upon an unspoken presupposition. In effect we say: If this is a right-angled triangle, the square on the hypotenuse is equal to the sum of the squares on the other two sides. In all such geometric figures, we presuppose something without which the proof is not valid. Because we do not refer to experience, we do not require an exact figure; for we derive the geometric cognition from the exemplary construction of our thoughts, regardless of whether the actual figure in front of us is completely congruent with it. In geometry, the human mind is concerned with its own ideal productions, of which real figures and diagrams are only imperfect symbols.

Therefore, as geometry proves, cognition of the world need not necessarily be the product of experience, of the mere functioning of our senses; from them we certainly obtain immediate intuitions or ideas; but, in themselves, these would be blind, dead things in relation to which our minds would be entirely passive. They contain the raw material of cognitions, but do not, by themselves, constitute cognitions. These blind intuitions become true cognitions through the active, productive activity of the mind, which, by means of thought, creates *concepts*.

Every science operates with concepts. But concepts are products of the human mind, of thought, which do not exist in reality. The concept 'triangle': a flat area bounded by three straight lines. A triangle possessing these characteristics *alone* is inconceivable; there are innumerable kinds of individual triangles, varying according to their sides and angles, but the concept as such is inconceivable and only exists by thought and for thought.

[1] Translator's note: Intuition (Ger. *Anschauung*), immediate apprehension through the senses without reasoning (Latin *intueri*, to look at or envisage).

The naïve person, that is the person whose attitude is not philosophic or critical, imagines the things of the world to be as he sees and experiences them, that he bears an image of the world within him, so to speak; but Kant has shown that we do not know at all what the object, the 'thing-in-itself', is, but only how it appears to us on the basis of the laws governing our intellectual constitution, which are present *a priori*,[1] from the first, and to which experiences are then added *a posteriori*.[2] 'That all our cognition begins with experience', observes Kant, 'cannot be doubted, for how else should the faculty of cognition be awakened into activity? In order of time, therefore, no cognition precedes experience and everything begins with the latter. That all our cognition starts *with* experience does not, however, imply that it originates *from* experience.'

Cognition, therefore, springs from two sources in collaboration, from the functioning of the senses and understanding (or, as Kant says, reason); objects are given us by the former, but *conceptually* thought by the latter. Without the senses we should not become aware of any object, but without understanding we should form no conception of it. 'Thoughts without content are empty, intuitions without concepts are blind.' It is therefore necessary to render concepts sensible by means of individual representations, but equally necessary to apprehend sensuous intuitions conceptually. Thus, we render the 'concept triangle' sensible by means of any actual triangle, remaining fully conscious that this particular triangle only *represents* the 'concept triangle', and that it could equally well be replaced by some other triangle.

All our intuitions are of a dual nature. On the one hand, objects appear to be outside ourselves and externally co-existent, i.e. in space. On the other, they seem to exist within our own minds, either *simultaneously* or *in succession*, hence, therefore, in time. Thus, *space* and *time* are the two forms to which all our

---

[1] *a priori* does not imply innate; *a priori* cognitions are those which come into being independently of experience.

[2] *a posteriori* cognitions are empirical cognitions, having their source in experience.

intuitions are bound, and since they are ideas directly related to objects, they are themselves intuitions. But the reason why all our intuitions are bound up with precisely these two forms must lie in the manner in which our faculty of imagination receives the impression of objects, in other words, in the primary nature of our minds themselves. Space and time, therefore, are pure intuitions, present *a priori* in advance of any real sensation, inherent in the faculty of imagination of our souls, and underlie all our real sensations as necessary preconditions of their possibility. For this very reason, however, space and time are not something appertaining to objects themselves, but are merely subjective ideas within ourselves.

Thus, space and time—however strange this may seem to naïve, i.e. non-critical, thinkers—are only necessary ideas *a priori*, underlying all intuitions. Every objective idea which we have experienced, we 'project' spatially on to a place in the outer world; this is a necessary and universal function of the human mind. That the idea of space stems *a priori* and not from experience is clear from the fact that space is 'infinite', which no one can experience or demonstrate. Furthermore, it is possible to conceive the complete absence of things from space, but not the absence of space itself. Space is not a universal concept of the relationship of things in general, but a pure (i.e. stemming from thought) intuition, a necessary mode of intuition *a priori*.

However, we should not overlook the fact that Kant is not concerned with the problem of the genesis of the idea or intuition of space in the course of intellectual development, of the manner in which it evolves in the child; this is a question for psychology. In his critique of cognition, Kant is investigating the finished product.

The spatial arrangement of the things of the outer world is, thus, a creation of our minds. Out of the vast number of sensations from the outer world, the human mind constructs a co-ordinate, spatial picture. Spatial pictures are products of the faculty of intuition.

Time also is no empirical (derived from experience) concept. It neither exists in its own right, nor is it attached to things as an objective determinant. Time is nothing but the form of the inner sense, i.e. of the intuition of ourselves and our inward condition. Simultaneity or temporal succession could not be perceived, without the pre-existence of the idea of time, *a priori*. Time is a necessary idea, underlying all intuitions. As with space, it is possible to conceive the absence of phenomena from time, but not the absence of time itself, which, therefore, is given *a priori*. Past, present, and future do not appertain to things themselves, but only indicate the relation in which things stand to ourselves. Time arranges our experiences in sequence, it cannot be perceived itself, but only that which happens in it. Time—like space—has no beginning and no end, how could the idea of it stem from experience? Our minds are simply possessed from the first, *a priori*, of the capacity to register our experiences temporally.

The basic idea of Kant's philosophic theory of cognition, which he consistently pursues, is that our minds are living, actively operative organisms, drawing the material for their functioning from without, through the senses and through experience, but shaping this substance autonomously, according to their own laws and, hence, forming their cognition themselves.

However strange and absurd it may appear to the naïve (the non-critical) to say: The understanding is itself the well-spring of the laws of nature, the understanding does not derive the laws *from* nature, but prescribes them *to* nature. Kant, nevertheless, convincingly demonstrates that it is the active functioning of our minds themselves which establishes these laws on the basis of the vast number of outer impressions. The order which rules in the world, and rests upon the principles of cause and effect, has its foundations in our thinking, which, by organizing our cognitions, leads to the sciences. The general principles of the sciences originate from the laws of thought, from the constitution of our minds.

The 'eternal, immutable, high laws, which govern every step along the circle of our lives' (Goethe: *The Divine*), are not won from mere experience; the active formative efficiency of the human mind has imparted this shape to the substance of the innumerable multitude of individual impressions. Kant is the

Copernicus of philosophy. 'Hitherto', he observes, 'it has been assumed that all our cognition must conform to objects, that is to outer experience; but all attempts at establishing, *a priori* by means of concepts, fresh facts about objects, and so extending our cognition, have, on the basis of this presupposition, proved fruitless. We should, therefore, test the possibility that we should make better advances in the tasks of metaphysics (here, the critical theory of cognition, cognition from pure reason, pure understanding) by assuming that *objects* must conform to our *cognition*. This procedure would resemble the initial hypotheses of Copernicus, who, failing to arrive at a satisfactory explanation of the movements of the heavenly bodies on the assumption that they revolved round the observer, tried whether he might not meet with greater success by taking the observer as revolving and the stars as remaining at rest.'

However, it does not suffice the human mind merely to give to the impressions which reach it through the senses their proper places in space-time. The development of unitary cognition out of the chaotic confusion of sensations and perceptions requires the latter to be linked together by concepts (synthesis). All impressions are judged according to certain rules, whose validity is assumed *a priori*, quite apart from experience. Kant names, in all, twelve such connective concepts or categories of thought. These are the basic forms of the elaboration in thought of the material of cognition. They include: unity, multiplicity, causality, possibility. It is not necessary to our purposes to enumerate them all. The following examples will show the function of these categories. Things in themselves possess neither unity nor multiplicity, neither are they subject to the causal relationship; we ourselves, through the operation of our understanding, combine certain impressions *a priori* into a unity or a multiplicity (trunk, branches, twigs, leaves into the concept tree); further, we ourselves confirm the existence of causal relationships, of causes and effects (thunder, lightning). According to Kant, the cognition of causal relations, of cause and effect, is equally *a priori*, being determined by the constitution of our minds. The position here is analogous to that regarding space and time. Every cause must have a further cause, producing a causal series without beginning or end which, being infinite, cannot stem from experience and can only be the outcome of thought. The categories are only applicable to phenomena within our consciousness. Hence, it is we who prescribe laws to nature, not she who gives them to us. As in mathematics, so in the natural sciences, the human mind moves among structures of its own creation. Our constructive understanding builds up the world from the sum total of impressions, according to its own laws of thought; our world-picture, therefore, is not an image of reality, precisely corresponding to the original. We cannot know, and can never learn the nature of the world 'in itself'.

Naturally, this does not imply that we only move in an illusory and schematic world. Let us clearly understand the Kantian conception of nature. There must be *some* connection between sensibility and understanding, between the outer and the inner world. This is already proved by the possibility of experiment in the natural sciences. The results of reflection and calculation can be tested practically by experiment. Hence, there must exist common ground between the sensuous world and the understanding.

But are there also universal and necessary cognitions of *super-sensory* things? Is there a metaphysical world beyond reality, beyond sensory perceptions and cognitions? Is the existence of God susceptible of proof, or is this only a matter of belief? What of immortality and free-will?

Certainly such things can be thought, but not rendered sensible. Super-sensory things are only thinkable or 'intelligible', i.e. they are objects which can only be represented by the intelligence and are not derived from any sensory intuitions. Yet there must be something intrinsic to the constitution of the human mind which leads to the ever-repeated preoccupation, in theology as in philosophy, with super-sensory things, and even to attempts at the establishment of a 'science' of the super-sensory.

Awareness of the connection between the phenomena of the inner life and cognition, of the fact that the individual phenomena form an absolute whole, led to the notion of a bearer of this unitary inner life, to the supposition of a *soul*.

According to Kant, reason, recognizing the connection between external phenomena, draws the conclusion that the things of the outer world must also form an absolute whole and have an ultimate cause. This reflection leads to the notion of the *universe*. But inner and outer world, soul and nature, together cause the assumption of an ultimate common basis, embracing both of them. This leads reason to the notion of *God*, who holds and unites everything.

However, nothing can rationally be predicated concerning the soul; for the life of the soul never makes its appearance as a totality. The understanding only apprehends individual experiences in space and time and cannot, therefore, demonstrate the unity of the inner life, but, according to Kant, reason is bound to presuppose it.

And even though the supposition of a universe is an absolute necessity to the reason, we cannot form a judgment about it, because the universe is not, for us, a given object, but only an inference of reason. We could only form a judgment concerning the universe if it were present to our intuitions. But it is not. The universe as a unit is merely a notion originating in reason, with no basis in experience; it leads to insoluble contradictions, as we shall explain.

The concept of a unitary universe implies that this universe has a boundary. But in that case, something must be thought to exist beyond this boundary; for a boundary presupposes a space on either side of it. But what would then become of the universe? But if we suppose the world to be without end, this would be a mere phrase; for we cannot perceive infinite space. Thus, the universe merely answers a need of reason and is a contradictory and hence impossible idea.

The same applies to the question of whether the world has a beginning in time. We cannot take any point of time in the past, without immediately thinking that something must already have existed prior to it. But time without end is inconceivable. Space and time are simply forms of our thought.

The notion of God stems equally from a need of reason. There are no rational proofs of the existence of God. Theoretically, the existence of God can be neither proved nor refuted. According to Kant, God is a notion, a useful and necessary notion, to which reason requires us to cling. 'The ideal of the highest Being is nothing else than a regulative principle of reason to regard all connection in the world *as if* it arose from an all-sufficient, necessary cause, in order, in the process of explaining the latter, to arrive at the rule of a systematic unity, necessitated by universal laws; it is not an assertion of an existence necessary in itself. *God is not a being outside me, but merely a thought within me.*' The critique of reason in no way strives to deny the existence of God, it only denies our cognition of it—and then only our theoretical cognition. If God's being is to be expressed in any affirmative manner, this can only be through conceiving God as the basis of the world's moral order, as the moral author of the world and as the world's ethical purpose.

We are, therefore, compelled to believe in God and immortality, not for theoretical, but for practical reasons; no science and no intelligence will ever succeed in demonstrating the untenability of these notions. God, freedom and immortality are inevitable propositions of pure reason. Reason impels us to act '*as if*' God and immortality were facts. 'There can never have lived a man of integrity', writes Kant in *Dreams of a Spirit-Seer*, 'capable of tolerating the thought that everything comes to an end with death, and whose noble spirit did not rise to the hope of a future. . . . To those thirsters after knowledge, who seek so urgently to unlock the secrets of the other world, we can make the simple, but very natural answer that they would be well advised to possess themselves in patience until they get there. But since our fate in the world to come may be, to a great extent, determined by the manner in which we have discharged our duties in this one, I will end upon the words with which Voltaire makes his honest Candide conclude, after so much scholastic disputation: Let us look after our happiness and go into the garden and work!'

3

Kant's Ethic

IN THE *Critique of Pure Reason* Kant attempted a scientific analysis of cognition and the determination of its limits. In his *Critique of Practical Reason* (1788) he enquires into the will of 'faculty of desire', in other words into morality, the world of volition and action. It deals with the questions: Under what circumstances must an action be universally recognized as good? By what criteria is human volition to be judged and evaluated? In what does the ethical personality consist?

Before we can go into Kant's doctrine of morality, we must briefly indicate some of the fundamental problems of ethics.

Ethically speaking, an action may be judged from two viewpoints. On the one hand, it may be characterized as ethical or good if its general *consequences* are good; but, on the other hand, an action will also be called good if it proceeds from good *motives*, from an ethical *intention*. We therefore discriminate between the *ethic of consequences* and the *ethic of intention*. Now, it is naturally easier to observe the consequences of an action than to recognize its motives. Moreover, good intentions may produce unhappy results, while evil intentions may result in good. A philanthropist may be motivated by the egoistic desire to win recognition and respect, but be credited with an ethical sentiment which, in reality, is entirely absent. Judgment of an action by its consequences or by its motives is, therefore, a highly uncertain procedure, very liable to error.

Pre-eminent among motives of human conduct are the emotions. Benevolence, pity, sympathy, love impel to good actions. Repercussions upon the doer include self-satisfaction, self-esteem and a feeling of blissfulness, which appear as a purpose in life and constitute a stimulus to further conduct of the same nature. On superficial consideration, that conduct appears to man to be good which contributes to his feeling of bliss, to his *inner* happiness. But according to Kant, bliss is not the highest value or the true determinant of man. Against this assumption his ethical consciousness revolts. 'We find', he states, 'that the more a cultivated reason is devoted to the aim of enjoying life and happiness, the farther the man strays from true contentment.'

The conduct of a religious person is determined by the precepts and commandments of his religion, which confronts him with the prospect of eternal reward for obedience to them or punishment for disobedience.

All the foregoing ethical conceptions were vigorously opposed by Kant. He wishes, above all, that volition and conduct shall be kept clear of emotions and, at the same time, repudiates the intervention of religion; for which of the various religions is to be taken as a universally valid determinant of ethical principles? Ethical norms should not be determined by considerations of future bliss; these would be egoistical and therefore non-ethical ends.

Ethical views must rest upon certain principles. Kant's fundamental ethical principle runs:

'*There is nothing in the world which can be unreservedly regarded as good, except a good will.*'

Thus, the highest value is not inner happiness or bliss, but good will; the value of a human life is not to be measured by the amount of happiness it brought, but by the extent to which the individual gave evidence of good will.

But how is good will to be recognized? Good will is present when volition and conduct spring, not from fear or inclination, but from the consciousness of *duty*. *Do your duty* is, for Kant, the highest ethical precept. Under all circumstances man should do what seems to him to be his duty, regardless of all other inducements, considerations and emotions, regardless of whether it is to his own advantage or disadvantage.

Man should not be concerned with whether his conduct will make him more or less happy, but that he at all times does his duty. Every thinking man feels within him this unconditional ethical demand, this *'categorical* (absolutely valid) *imperative'* (command), which bids him, free from all sensual desires, to do only that which he has accepted as right and good. In popular terms, this categorical imperative or inner command is the voice of conscience.

'Conscience is the awareness of an inner seat of judgment within man', says Kant, 'before which his thoughts arraign one another and defend themselves. Every man possesses a conscience and feels that an inner judge is watching and threatening him and compelling his respect (a combination of esteem with fear); this guardian of the law within him is not something he has formed of his own free will, but is incorporate in his being. It follows him like his shadow when he thinks to flee it. He can, indeed, stupefy himself or put himself to sleep with the aid of pleasures and dissipations, but he cannot avoid an occasional clearing of his mind or awakening, upon which he immediately hears conscience's awful voice. In the extreme of depravity he can reach a point at which he pays no further heed to it, but he can never avoid *hearing* it.'[1]

The roots of the consciousness of duty are to be sought in respect for ethical law. In Kant's view, only those actions have moral value which proceed from respect for ethical law, from the categorical imperative of duty. Act according to such principles as you could wish to be erected into universal law, in such a manner, therefore, as you could wish all men to act. Never act in despite of your conscience. Never act in a manner detrimental to the dignity of man. The moral man feels his guiding principles, his high value and his human dignity to be sublime.

According to Kant, universally valid ethical law *does not stem from experience*, but is *inherent* in reason itself, *a priori*. The suppo-

---

[1] In *Tasso* Goethe makes the princess say:

> 'Quite softly speaks a god within our breast,
> Quite softly, but quite perceptibly, he shows us,
> What we should grasp, what we should flee. . . .'
>   (*Tasso*, Act 3, Scene 1)

sition of unconditional free will is a necessary precondition of Kant's ethical doctrine. Freedom of the will is a necessary stipulation for morality. And even if it is not capable of proof, it must nevertheless be presupposed in the world of mind. Man feels impelled by an inner force to act against his inclinations, against his sensual instincts, and to do that which is better. The moral personality consists in freedom and independence from egoistic tendencies and in striving to subordinate the sensual element of the nature to the spiritual. Honest self-examination will usually show us whether our actions in particular cases proceeded from mere inclination or from duty. In Kant's view, actions which spring from emotions, from love, benevolence, affection, are devoid of moral value. Not that he regards them as ethically objectionable. He remarks somewhere: 'It is very fine to do good out of love of mankind or sympathetic benevolence, or to be just out of love of order, but in so doing we have not yet reached the true moral maxim of our behaviour. . . . Duty and obligation are the sole appellations to be bestowed upon our relation to moral law.' It is often impossible for us to feel love for certain people, feelings cannot be compelled, but always and everywhere we can do our duty, regardless of our inclinations, even towards our enemies, although it be with a cold heart. Ethical conduct proceeding from duty rests, as it were, on a firm foundation, whereas conduct based on inclination, on mere sentiment, is fortuitous.

Before the simple questions and problems of everyday life, it is generally not difficult to see what our duty is. But there are many human situations in which the decision of conscience is not such a simple matter, where the individual is confronted by two simultaneous and incompatible sets of duties and can only fulfil one set at the expense of the other. Kant simply cannot tell us wherein our duty consists in every case, because individual circumstances and conditions are always different; it is therefore impossible to lay down universally valid rules and injunctions or to erect an obligatory ethical code.

Kant has been charged with 'Rigourism', because he only ascribes moral value to actions proceeding from a sense of duty. Thus Schiller, in his poem *The Philosophers*, where he writes:

Scruple of Conscience:

I like rendering services to my friends, but unfortunately I do so out of affection,
I am therefore gnawed by doubts as to whether I am virtuous.

Decision:

There is nothing else for it, you must seek to despise them
And then do with distaste as duty enjoins you.

But Schiller, who was strongly attached to Kant's ideas, has here misunderstood the Königsberg philosopher. Kant would have answered his objection: If I only render services to my friends 'out of' affection, in consequence of my emotional attitude towards them, that is all very well, but is of no ethical value, any more than the action of a mother in sacrificing herself for her child would be; for in this she would be driven by a natural instinct, which appears even in animals. But if I also serve my friends 'with' affection, this is in no way incompatible with my doing so out of duty as well. Thus, inclination and duty may well go hand in hand. The true moral value of our conduct is most easily recognized when inclination and duty are in contradiction, when we do good and exhibit good will towards a man who is repugnant to us, towards whom we feel no sort of affection.

Schiller's ethical ideal consists in the harmony of duty with inclination, which he sees as the distinguishing mark of the 'beautiful soul'; but Kant would like to subordinate inclination completely to the stern commandments of duty. He does not believe that duty and inclination can, in every case, be brought into concordance. But even one's duty can be done with a cheerful heart and without reluctance. A fair-minded interpretation of the Kantian ethic, therefore, hardly justifies its being described as rigorous. His ethical doctrine opposes the flaccid eudaemonist morality of his time and merely demands the liberation of ethical sentiment and ethical volition from the motives of the promotion of happiness. According to Kant, nothing can be termed ethical except volition out of pure respect for moral law, free from the influence of inclinations, moods, sensual impulses, of sympathy or antipathy.[1]

In the last analysis, Kant's views on ethics are founded in his personality, in his own mental make-up. For his success in life he had largely to thank his inflexible energy and his iron will, which enabled him to bring his projects to realization. This emphasis on will-power also finds expression in his ethical ideas. Kant was ruled, not by feeling, but most definitely by intelligence. The benevolence which he showed his fellow-men, even his nearest relatives, sprang far less from his heart than from his sense of moral duty. The categorical imperative of duty seemed to him the highest ethical law, irreversibly valid for everyman. His own character-traits: stoic apathy, self-control, conscientious and faithful obedience to the injunctions of morality, all contributed to his conception of life and strongly influenced his ethical doctrine. If man follows, not his humours and pleasures, but only moral law, the voice of conscience, he rises to a level of dignity, regardless of his outer circumstances and social position, such as can never be attained by him who pursues only his own happiness.

The extent to which the will can govern and dominate the body, Kant demonstrated in the conduct of his own life. In spite of his feeble physical constitution, he wrung from nature a long life and a tireless capacity for work. The precepts of his treatise *On the Power of the Mind to Master Morbid Feelings by Resolution Alone* he carried out with success in his own case. By exercise, continued right into old age, he compelled his puny body to obey the commands of his will; similarly, he consistently disciplined his inner nature and guided his conduct by principles, never by humours or the 'weather in his soul'. In every respect he lived what he taught, his philosophy and his conduct of life were in concord.

[1] The aesthetician Friedrich Theodor Vischer (1807-87) puts similar views into the mouth of his Albert Einhart in *Also One*, who observes: moral law rises like 'a second story above human nature'. Here there is no option, here one does not enquire after pleasure and unpleasure, here option is subject to stern laws, laws which are unconditional and timeless truth; and everyone who claims the title of moral being must accept the dominion of these laws without reserve.

The effects of Kant's ethical writings were of much greater importance and more enduring than those of his theory of cognition. His exegeses and his conviction of free ethical self-determination made a deep and widespread impression.

In a letter about Kant to his friend Vogel (13th July 1788), Jean Paul wrote enthusiastically: 'For heaven's sake buy two books: Kant's *Critique of Practical Reason* and Kant's *Fundamental Principles of the Metaphysics of Morals*. Kant is not a light of the world, but a whole radiant solar system in one.'

As in his theory of cognition, Kant—and this should be noted—investigates the *finished article* of ethical consciousness; he is not concerned with the evolution of ethics, with the course of man's ethical development; this leads him to assume a categorical imperative *a priori*, a compulsion of conscience, an autonomous, law-giving essence. The ethical will of reason in the individual, as in the collective whole, promulgates its laws, which he accepts and which he must obey if he wishes to preserve his dignity as a man.

A critical *psychological* investigation into the genesis of ethical views shows conscience, the ethical predisposition, to be capable, to a certain extent, of being fashioned and developed. It disproves the existence of an *a priori*, absolute moral sense and shows the ethical person, social man, to be the late product of a slow evolutionary process. It demonstrates that there is no such thing as an absolute ethic, everywhere and universally valid, and that the conception of what constitutes duty varies greatly according to time, place and custom. For this reason, Kant had to content himself with the purely *formal* determination of the ethical, by the erection of the categorical imperative of duty, without expounding its *content*, which would have been quite impossible.

The capacity of the ethical predisposition to be moulded and developed is dependent upon man's intelligence and judgment and his capacity to experience emotions with greater or lesser intensity and then relive them within himself; out of this inner process he fashions impulses and inhibitions to action. Kant looks upon this as an admissible, but not a moral standpoint. The atrophying of this predisposition may lead to moral insanity.

Kant, a relief by P. H. Collin, 1782

Kant, a painting from the Dresden «Kunsthandel»,
about 1790

A man of weak intellect and blunted emotions is, therefore, capable of developing only a very limited conscience; hence, he will only arrive at a very inadequate comprehension of his duty, in him the categorical imperative will make itself felt to a lesser degree than in a man of finer and more highly organized mental structure.

But Kant's great deed consists in his having opposed, in his ethic, self-seeking and the pursuit of happiness and having won recognition for the concept of inexorable duty. His morality rests, not upon states of mind, inclinations and self-interest, but upon firm principles and inviolate commandments. 'It is certain', wrote Schiller to Körner (18th February 1793), 'that nothing greater can be said of mortal man, than this dictum of Kant's which is at the same time the very essence of his whole philosophy: Determine your life from within yourself!'

Pestalozzi was expressing similar views when he said: 'Of course, circumstances often make men, but I saw at once: in his case the man makes the circumstances; he has within him the power to guide them along the path chosen by his will. He possesses the inner power, unhampered by sensual desires, to contribute to his own inward ennoblement and attain to the level of true humanity.' Pestalozzi arrived at this insight without any influence from Kant; he never read the latter's works. But when he heard of Kant's ideology through conversations with Fichte, who spent 1793-4 in Zürich, he was astonished by the extent to which it accorded with his own.[1] Both Kant and Pestalozzi hold to the view that man can attain the dignity of true humanity through *self-determination.*

Through establishing and stressing the concept of immutable, irreversible duty, Kant exercised a powerful influence over the formation of the national character.

---

[1] On 16th January 1794, Pestalozzi wrote to Philipp Emanuel von Fellenberg: 'Fichte is reviewing *Lienhard and Gertrud* in the light of the Kantian philosophy. . . . I am delighted to have been convinced, through conversations with Fichte, that the path of my own experience has brought me close to the findings of the philosophy of Kant.'

4

From Kant's Moral Teaching[1]

Good Will

THERE IS NOTHING we can think of in the whole world, or indeed outside it, which can be unreservedly looked upon as good, except a good will. Intelligence, wit, the power of judgment and all the rest of the talents of the intellect, or courage, determination and fixity of purpose as qualities of temperament are undoubtedly good and desirable in many respects; but these natural gifts may also become extremely evil and noxious in the service of a will, whose specific construction is, for this reason, called character, which is not good. The case is similar with the gifts of fortune. Power, wealth, honour, even health and that state of well-being and contentment with one's lot that goes by the name of happiness, give courage, which, where there is no good will to guide it into beneficent and purposeful channels of thought and action, often degenerates into pride.

Moderation in emotions and passions, self-discipline and sober reflection seem not merely good in their results, but even appear to constitute an integral part of the person's inner worth; but it is far from possible to declare them unreservedly good (in spite of the absolute value placed upon them by the ancients). For without the principles of a good will they may become highly evil; the cold-bloodedness of a villain not only renders him far more dangerous, but also altogether more detestable in our eyes than he would have seemed without this characteristic.

Good will is not to be valued by what it effects or achieves, by its ability to attain any particular set purpose. The specific good-

[1] According to the Academy Edition of Kant's Collected Works: vol. iv, *Fundamental Principles of the Metaphysics of Morals*, p. 393 ff.; vol. vi, *Metaphysical First Principles of Moral Philosophy*, p. 429 ff., 453.

ness of the volition itself is incomparably more valuable than anything it may bring about in the interests of any one inclination, or, indeed, of the sum total of all inclinations. Even if a particularly ill-disposed destiny or a step-motherly niggardliness on the part of nature has entirely deprived this will of the faculties needed for the realization of its intentions; even if its greatest endeavours achieve nothing, leaving only good will (not in the sense of a mere wish, but of the application of all the forces at our disposal): It would still shine like a jewel on its own, as something containing within it its full value. Neither utility nor fruitlessness can add to or detract from this value. Practical achievement would, so to speak, be merely the setting enabling it to be handled more easily in general use or to attract the attention of those who are not yet sufficiently expert, but it would not recommend it to experts nor determine its value.

Duty

But the concept of a good will, valuable in itself independently of its purposes, such as attends a sound intelligence and requires enlightenment rather than teaching, this concept, which is always the prime criterion in estimating the whole value of our actions and which determines all the others, demands further elaboration. To this end we will consider the concept of duty, which contains that of a good will, albeit with certain subjective reservations and impediments, but is far from concealing and disguising the latter. Its effect is rather to make good will stand out all the more clearly by contrast.

In this context, I shall pass over all actions which are recognizably contrary to duty, although useful in one respect or another. The question of whether they spring from duty does not arise, since they actually conflict with it. I shall also leave aside those actions which are really enjoined by duty, to which men have no direct inclination, but which they nevertheless carry out under the impulsion of some quite different inclination. It is far more difficult to observe the difference where an action is one of duty, but the subject has an additional *direct* inclination to it. For instance, it is certainly the shopkeeper's duty not to overcharge inexperienced customers; where there is plenty of business, the clever skopkeeper does not do so, but keeps to a fixed price for everyone, so that even a child may safely buy from him. He therefore gives *honest* service. But this is far from indicating that the merchant's conduct is dictated by duty and honest principles. It is demanded by his own best interests. There is also no reason to suppose that, in addition, he feels an affection for his customers which precludes him from offering advantageous prices to any one of them as compared with the rest. The action is, therefore, the result neither of duty nor of direct inclination, but merely of self-interest.

To be philanthropic, wherever possible, is a duty, in addition to which there are many sympathetically inclined souls who, without any other motivation of vanity or self-interest, find an inner pleasure in spreading joy and take a delight in the satisfaction of others, in so far as it is their work. But it is my contention that such acts, however admirable and in accordance with duty they may be, have no true moral value, but are on a par with other inclinations, such, for instance, as the inclination to win honour; when, by good fortune, the latter leads to actions in conformity with duty and the common good, it is thereby worthy of respect and deserves praise and encouragement, but is of no high intrinsic value; for the maxim of moral content is lacking, namely that such actions should be done, not from inclination, but from duty. Let us assume, therefore, that the spirit of our philanthropist was clouded over by his own griefs, which extinguished all sympathy with the fates of others, that he was still capable of doing good to other sufferers, whose misery, however, did not move him because he was fully preoccupied with his own; assume now that, devoid of all impelling inclination, he wrenched himself free from this mortal insensibility and carried out his philanthropic act entirely without inclination, exclusively from duty, only then would it acquire genuine moral value. Furthermore: if nature has put little sympathy into the heart of a particular man, if he (in other respects an honourable man) is by temperament cold and indifferent to the sufferings of others—perhaps because he is endowed with exceptional patience and fortitude with regard to his own, and supposes or demands the same of others; if nature has not exactly fashioned a philanthropist out of such a man (who would indeed not be the worst of her products), would he not then discover within him a source from which to draw for himself a far higher value than that of a good-natured temperament? Of course! For the moral, and incomparably highest worth of a character begins at precisely that point where philanthropy springs, *not from inclination* (sympathy), *but from duty.*

Lying

The greatest injury a man can inflict on his duty towards himself is a lie. This may be outward or inward. The former renders him an object of contempt in the eyes of others, but the latter renders him such in his own eyes, which is much worse. It wounds the dignity of mankind in the person of the liar; the injuries which may thereby be caused to others do not constitute the specific quality of the vice, which would then consist merely in the violation of his duty to his fellow-men, a question that does not arise here; nor does it consist in the injury he inflicts upon himself. No, lying amounts, rather, to the abandonment and destruction of his human dignity. It may be the result of mere thoughtlessness, or even of good nature; nevertheless, to cede to it is a crime against man's own person and a baseness which is bound to render the perpetrator contemptible in his own sight.

Such, for instance, would be the assertion of belief in a future judge of the world, based, not on any inner conviction, but merely on the view that it can do no harm and might be useful to give credence to a 'God which knoweth the heart', in order to win his favour by a sham—to be on the safe side. Or if a man, not being in any doubt as to the existence of God, should flatter himself with inwardly respecting his law, merely because he feels within him no other motive force than fear of punishment.

Philanthropy

Philanthropy, i.e. doing all in one's power to effect the happiness of others who are in need, without thought of personal advantage, is the duty of everyone.

For everyone, being himself in distress, hopes for help from others. But if he were to proclaim, as a principle, his unwilling-ness to render assistance to others in distress, everyone else, when he was in trouble, would similarly refuse him their aid or, at least, be justified in refusing it.

Philanthropy, in the case of a philanthropist who is wealthy, is a duty almost entirely devoid of merit, if it simultaneously places the recipient under an obligation. The pleasure derived by the philanthropist from his action, which costs him no per-sonal sacrifice, is a kind of wallowing in moral sentiment. He must carefully avoid the appearance of thinking to place the recipient under an obligation, since this would, by abasing the latter in his own eyes, withdraw all true philanthropy from the action. He must rather look upon himself as obliged, or hon-oured, by the acceptance, indicating that he is merely acting upon the injunctions of duty, if he cannot carry out his philanthropic act in secret (which is the best). This virtue is greater when the means to philanthropy are limited, and the philanthropist is strong enough to take upon himself, in silence, the ill from which he is sparing others; then he is really to be regarded as *morally rich.*

5

From Kant's Philosophy of Life

The Three Endowments of the Soul

THE THREE ENDOWMENTS of the soul are a sound intelligence, a merry heart and a free, self-governing will. If to these we add a healthy body which will aid the intelligence by its senses, the emotions of the heart by its vitality and the will by its activity, we have all the inner endowments.

The True Value of Life

It is easy enough to assess the value of life to us, if this is estimated merely by what we *enjoy*. It falls below zero; for who would care to begin life over again under the same conditions, or even according to a new plan of his own that was still based merely on enjoyment? Thus, there is nothing left but the value which we *ourselves give* to our lives by what we not only *do*, but do to purposes so independent of nature, that the very existence of nature is only given a purpose by our actions.

True Happiness

Happiness is the universal watchword, but it is not to be found anywhere in nature; the best man can achieve is to *merit* happiness. Only in what he *does*, not in what he *enjoys* or suffers, only in the self which is independent of his nature and not fashioned by destiny, can he find contentment.

Preserve True Human Dignity

Let men not become slaves! Let not your rights be spurned beneath the feet of others! Contract no debts for which you cannot give full security. Accept no charity you can do without and be neither parasites nor sycophants nor, which differs from these only in degree, beggars. For this reason, be thrifty to avoid poverty. Complaint and whining are unworthy of you, especially when you are aware that you yourselves are at fault.

Against Fawning

Fawning among men is unworthy. He who makes himself a worm cannot complain if he is trodden underfoot. Bowing and scraping before another is in every case unworthy of a man.

Of Self-Deception

The dishonesty of humbugging oneself, which hinders the establishment of a genuine moral attitude, spreads outward into falsity and the deception of others which, if it is not to be called malice, at least deserves the name of unworthiness. It belongs to that which is evil in human nature, to the rotten flaw in our race

FROM KANT'S PHILOSOPHY OF LIFE

which, until we have rooted it out, will prevent the seed of goodness from developing, as it otherwise would.

Lying

The greatest injury which man can inflict upon his duty towards himself, looked upon purely as a moral being, is the opposite of truthfulness: *lying*. This is the abandonment and, as it
were, destruction of his human dignity.

Work

Work is the best way of enjoying life. In a state of health, the
greatest pleasure of the senses is rest after work. He who does
not work is never invigorated and gratified.

Improve Instead of Regretting

What cannot be altered must be cast from the mind: for it is
senseless to want to undo that which is done. To improve oneself is feasible and a duty; but to want to improve what is beyond
my power is absurd. The self-tormentor's penance, instead of a
swift change of heart leading to better conduct, is a pure waste of
effort; it has the added bad consequence that he feels his guilt to
have been atoned by mere repentance and spares himself the
effort, which reason should now urge him to redouble, to improve.

Sustain and Abstain

To husband one's powers and emotions too carefully weakens
and destroys them. It brings about a gradual extinction of the
life-force through lack of exercise, just as it may be exhausted by
too frequent and excessive use. Stoicism,[1] as a dietetic[2] principle
(*sustine et abstine*, sustain and abstain), therefore, has a place in
practical philosophy, not merely as a doctrine of virtue, but also
as therapeutics. The latter is philosophical, when the power of
men's reason to give them mastery over their sensual feelings,
by means of a self-given principle, determines their mode of life.

[1] The Stoics saw the highest good in the greatest possible freedom from
needs.
[2] Dietetics=art of living (Greek *diaita*, way of life).

Hope and Fear

To nourish oneself on hopes is unmanly, it is childish. Hope deprives us of the present itself through impatience, fear deprives us of its enjoyment.

The safest thing is to expect nothing great and to know in advance that one will adapt and accustom oneself to everything.

Character

A man whose actions have no fixed principle and, hence, no uniformity, has no character. Such a man may have a good heart, yet no character, because he is dependent upon his impulses and does not act according to maxims, to principles. Character calls for constancy and unity of principles.

6

Kant and Religion

KANT, as explained earlier, grew up in a very pious household. His mother, a woman of gentle nature and genuine religious feeling, used to take him with her, from an early age, on her regular visits to F. A. Schultz's prayer meetings. When they went for walks together, she continually drew his attention to the 'works of God' and awakened in him 'awe of the creator of all things'. These impressions of his early youth were never quite extinguished in Kant. During his eight years' residence at the Collegium Fredericianum he was powerfully influenced by the spirit of Pietism, which held particularly marked sway over that institution.

But in spite of the prolonged after-effect of his early religious upbringing, he later turned away more and more from biblical Christianity. He went to church only when his academic position required him to do so on some special occasion. Kant's philosophical convictions led him to reject, in particular, all the mystical element in religion, i.e. the emotional-intuitive submergence into the supersensory. 'If ever a man's religious opinions were cold declarations of reason; if ever a man eliminated from his religious practices anything which could be called emotion and repudiated all communion with the supernatural world, either for the instruction of his understanding or the animation of his will; if there was ever a man whose divine service consisted solely in obedience to the laws of reason and a devotion to duty, purified from all sensuality, that man', reports his friend Jachmann, 'was Kant.'

In his major work on religious belief, *Religion within the Limits of Reason Alone* (1793), the then sixty-nine-years-old sage made a philosophical analysis of the problem of religion.

The philosophy of religion is the science of religion's fundamental principles; it is theory and critique; it investigates the nature, origin and significance of religion and its relation to culture and to the life of the mind.

In his book, therefore, Kant attempts a philosophical exposition of the religious doctrine of ecclesiastical Christianity and its reduction to purely rational beliefs. Everything inconsistent with a refined moral and philosophical consciousness, he discards.

What then is Kant's conception of religion?

'Religion is the law within us, given added force by a lawgiver and judge above us; it is a morality applied to the recognition of God; it is the recognition of all our duties as divine commandments.'

Kant seeks to render morality independent of religion; he gives it an autonomous status. Indeed, religion may and should be critically examined by the moral consciousness. That which is promulgated by the church as divine revelation or divine commandment, must also stand examination from the ethical viewpoint.

Kant will have nothing to do with the idea that, in religious experience, we are dealing with a special area of consciousness, in which, as Schleiermacher correctly perceived, feeling plays an essential part. He rejects the founding of religion on feeling, in principle. He was himself the very antithesis of an emotional character. Religion of mere sentiment, he remarks, leads neither to knowledge nor to morality, but at most to wild devotion and mysticism.

In Kant's view, it is not religion which leads to true morality, but vice versa, religion must itself proceed from morality. 'The moral law of reason is in concordance with the holy will of God; to know the latter we must interrogate the former.' The only possible and rational worship of God consists in doing the will of the Most High by faithful obedience to the commandments of reason. Moral religion is neither a mere cult, i.e. courting favour, nor false humility and contrition, but the good conduct of life. 'Everything which man does to please God, apart from living aright, is mere religious mania and the mock-service of God.'

Pestalozzi is subscribing to very similar views, when he makes the mother in *Lienhard and Gertrud* say to her weak-willed husband: 'My dear, weeping and falling on one's knees is nothing, but the determination to be honest and grateful towards God and man is everything! That one man is soft and the other less so is of no more consequence than the fact that one worm crawls into the dust with greater difficulty than the other.' Thus, the only indication of whether a man has religion lies in his obedience to his duties, as divine commandments.

Pure or moral religious belief, based on reason, is clearly different to historical ecclesiastical creeds rooted in revelation. Since man is weak, the latter obviously cannot be dispensed with entirely; but the church's creed ought to ascend ever nearer to the true divine service, in spirit and in truth. 'Religion built merely on theology can never contain any moral element. It will only give us fear of punishment on the one hand, and, on the other, profit-seeking aims and intentions (hope of reward in the life hereafter), resulting in a mere superstitious cult.' True religion must proceed from morality, and then be *followed* by theology. The value of religion is to be measured by the yardstick of its moral content. The church and its doctrine are significant only in the degree to which they contribute to the moral training of the human race.

Kant is passing judgment on all mere erudition in theology, when he writes: 'Once a religion has reached the point at which critical knowledge of ancient tongues and philosophical and antiquarian erudition constitute the foundations upon which it must be erected throughout all the ages and amongst all peoples, then the man most highly skilled in Greek, Hebrew, and so on, drags all orthodox believers along with him like children, however sour-faced they may look; in whatever direction he takes them, they may not utter a sound. . . . An erudite religion cannot be for all men; it must be possible for everyone to comprehend religion and base his convictions on common sense alone, which is very simply done in the case of purely moral religious belief.'

In Kant's view, the church tends to ascribe far too much significance to outward things, cult practices or mere faith in ecclesiastical dogmas and historical facts, which are entirely without influence on man's moral nature. By the acceptance of this kind of outward 'statutary' service of God, man comes to overvalue it; he then neglects the true service of God, *which consists in living aright*, and is content with outward things.

Kant had an entirely unecclesiastical attitude. Indeed, he may have felt a certain animosity against institutional religion, in consequence of the excess of 'pious ritual', penances, mortifications and devotional exercises, in which he was compelled to participate while attending the Latin school. The theologian Borowski, a member of the consistory, who revered the philosopher, regretted that he looked upon the Christian church merely as an 'institution to be tolerated for the sake of the weak'.

In Kant's view, the whole range of devotional practices are only of value as means of animating an effective piety and conscientious observance of duties as divine commandments. 'For the thesis that religion is no more than a kind of currying favour and ingratiation with the Most High, in regard to which men differ only by virtue of their varying opinions as to the mode of approach most likely to please Him, is madness. Whether it is determined by dogmas or not, such a view of religion undermines all moral conviction through its supposition of another method, besides the good life, of—as it were—sneaking into the Almighty's favour and making certain of a loophole in case of need.'

Kant attacks mere 'lip-service' and puts forward his own conception of prayer. Of the so-called 'means of grace', true prayer, in the philosopher's opinion, consists in the spirit, i.e. the moral attitude, from which it proceeds; but this moral attitude ought to accompany all our conduct, 'without cease, as though it took place in the service of God'. 'Therefore, we should not seek to find grace in the eyes of God by calling "Lord, Lord!", but by doing His will; that is, not by lauding him, but by living the good life.'

Although mere historical creeds are morally worthless, Kant nevertheless regards Christianity as the only 'public' religion which is truly moral; he is, therefore, at pains to present a *moral* exposition of the principal tenets of this religion, as is incumbent upon a 'purely philosophical religious doctrine, a religion within the limits of reason alone'. Thus Kant interprets 'belief in Christ', not as acceptance of the historical account of the life of Jesus, but as assimilation and striving after the ideal of the perfect man, God's well-beloved. Our true Comforter must be the consciousness of a good and pure attitude of mind, of a good will. Heaven and hell are only symbols of the morally good and morally evil.

And how about belief in miracles and prophecies? As mere 'repetition of incomprehensible things, it is entirely devoid of moral-religious value. Reasonable men do not believe in miracles in either practical or scientific life; they do not become any the more credible for being confined to the past.'

Ecclesiastical ritual, church services, baptism and holy communion are, in Kant's view, only symbols of moral community; true religiosity must be expressed in moral conduct. It is not religion's task to subjugate the will or the intelligence by means of any powers of this world or the next; its sole task is to strengthen the will to good. Moral religion does not consist in dogmas and rites, but in the disposition to observe all human duties as divine commandments.

In his exegeses, Kant exhibits a somewhat one-sided approach to the problem of religion, which he looks at from the moral standpoint only. He completely by-passes its psychological aspect, overlooking a very specific and primordial human predisposition and taking no account of the significance of religion to man's mental life and the whole of culture. But his thesis that the highest piety must be expressed in a moral life, and that all the rest of the outward religious behaviour, enjoined by revelation and the church, is of entirely secondary significance, is vitally important.

7

Kant on Christianity

THERE IS SOMETHING in Christianity which inspires our love, apart from the great respect irresistibly instilled by the sanctity of its laws. . . .

The aim of Christianity is: to promote a love of the whole business of the observance of duty. It succeeds in this, because its founder does not speak in imperious accents, demanding obedience to his will, but in the tone of a friend of men, urging upon his fellows the conduct which they would choose of their own free will, if they were true to the dictates of their understanding.

It is, therefore, the *liberal* manner of thought—equally far removed from servility and from unfettered licence—upon which Christianity depends for the effect of its doctrine, through which it is able to win men's hearts. It is the feeling of freedom of choice as to the final aim, which renders its legislation amiable. Although its teacher also proclaims the possibility of punishment,

[1] From: *On the Failure at all Philosophical Attempts at a Theodicy* (1791), Academy edition of Kant's Collected Works, vol. viii, p. 337 ff. ('By theodicy is to be understood the defence of the Creator's omniscience against the objection to it raised by reason, on account of the existence in the world of all that is contrary to His purposes.' Kant, loc. cit., p. 255.)

the latter is not to be understood as the motive force of compliance with its commandments; for then it would cease to be a teaching of love. This is only to be interpreted as a loving warning, springing from the lawgiver's benevolence, to guard against the harm which must inevitably befall the lawbreaker.

When Christianity promises rewards (for example, 'Be joyful and of good cheer, for everything shall be recompensed unto you in heaven'), according to the liberal way of thinking this must not be interpreted as an attempt to bribe men to good living; for in the latter case, Christianity would be lacking in love toward itself. It can only claim men's respect if the actions it requests from them are such as spring from altruistic motives; but without respect there is no true love. Therefore this promise should not be taken as implying that the rewards are to be the motivating factor of the actions. Love, which is the means of attaching a liberal way of thinking to a philanthropist, is not determined by the good received by the needy, but by the goodness of will of him who is desirous of dispensing it: even if he is not in a position to carry out his intentions, or is prevented from doing so by considerations involving the best interests of the world in general . . . .

If Christianity should ever cease to be a religion of love (which might well come to pass, if it cast aside its gentle spirit in favour of the weapon of peremptory authority), the minds of men would be filled with aversion and revolt against it, since there can be no neutrality in matters of morality; then Antichrist, regarded as the harbinger of the day of judgment, would begin his rule, which (although short) is likely to be founded upon fear and self-interest. But then, because Christianity was destined to be the universal religion, but not favoured by fate in becoming so, the (wrong) end of all things, morally speaking, would come about.

8

Kant as a Political Writer

KANT did not confine himself to investigating the ethical attitude appropriate to the individual, but also turned his interest to the life of the community, to the major problems of jurisprudence and politics. His essays, *On the Proverbial Saying: 'All very well in Theory but no Good in Practice* (1793); *Perpetual Peace* (1795); *Metaphysical First Principles of Jurisprudence* (1797) and *The Conflict of the Faculties* (Part 2) (1798) were all mainly devoted to questions of public life.

Kant's political views clearly showed the influence of Montesquieu and Rousseau, whose works he had studied closely. He also accorded full recognition to the unprejudiced spirit of Frederick the Great. The North Americans' war of liberation against their English oppressors (1776–83) aroused his particularly strong support, in consequence of his own marked sense of independence. This was the cause of his previously mentioned clash with the Englishman Joseph Green, who subsequently became his best friend (see page 41).

He followed with the greatest interest the developments of the French Revolution, carefully reading all the news about it given in the daily press. He found no history as instructive as that which he could read in the newspaper. 'Here I can see how everything comes into being, spreads and evolves,' he once stated. Current political events were a frequent topic of conversation with his friends at table. He regarded England's attitude as a serious obstacle to the development of political freedom in France. Great Britain's foreign policy, as pursued by her Secretary of State, William Pitt, seemed to him 'to be aimed at promoting slavery and barbarity, rather than liberty and culture'. In his pamphlet,

Kant, a miniature by C. Vernet, 1795

Kant, a bust by Fr. Hagemann, 1801

Perpetual Peace, which appeared in 1795, he stigmatizes the rapacious colonial policy of every nation, but is thinking primarily of England, summing up his judgment in the words: 'The English nation as a *people* is second to none as regards the relations of the individuals comprising it with one another, but as a *state* in relation to other states it is the most pernicious, tyrannical and warmongering of them all. To the English, the whole world is England and other countries and peoples merely their goods and chattels.'[1]

Kant would naturally have preferred things to have taken a more peaceful course in France. But although he was dismayed by the reign of terror and the outbursts of political passions, he nevertheless recognized the historical significance of these happenings. His future publisher, F. Nicolovius, reports that in 1794 Kant was still a complete democrat and of the opinion that all the atrocities which were being committed were insignificant in comparison with the lasting evil of despotism, which had previously existed in France, and that in all probability the Jacobins were right in their current actions.[2] The theologian, Abegg, whom we have mentioned before, who was a frequent visitor to Kant, noted in his diary (1st July 1798) that the latter was a wholehearted supporter of the French cause, and that all the outbreaks of immorality could not undermine his belief that representative government was best. Johann Schultz, the court chaplain, one of Kant's most convinced adherents, also observes in his diary at this period: 'He is an overt republican.'

In his tract, *The Conflict of the Faculties*, which was published in 1798, the philosopher writes enthusiastically of the events in France, of which he says: 'The revolution of a spirited people, which has taken place before our eyes, may succeed or come to nought, it may bring with it so much misery and horror that a man of good will could never take the decision to carry out the experiment for a second time at the same cost, even if he had good reason to hope for its success—this revolution, I say, nonetheless inspires in its beholders a sympathy bordering on en-

---

[1] *Loose Sheets from the Literary Remains*, vol. xv, no. 1366.
[2] *Memorial to G. H. L. Nicolovius*, by A. Nicolovius.

thusiasm. These happenings are not the phenomena of a revolution, but of the *evolution* of a social system based on natural rights, which will indeed not be established by bitter struggle alone, but toward which events are tending and which goes by the name of a republic.'[1]

A fundamental question of politics, which actively engaged Kant's attention, is how to unite the various individual wills into one general will, without abrogating the autonomy of each separate will, but instead giving it influence and recognition in a new sense. 'The will of all is the primal fount of all justice, and justice is the limitation of the liberty of each in the interest of the liberty of all, in so far as this can be achieved by a general system of laws.'

'A state is the unification of a mass of people by the acceptance of a set of legal statutes. The act by which the nation constitutes itself a state is the original contract or agreement by which each of its members gives up his outward freedom, to immediately re-assume it through his participation in the corporate whole, the nation regarded as a state.' It cannot therefore be said that, in the state, man has sacrificed *a part* of his inborn outer freedom to a purpose, observes Kant; for he has merely abandoned wild, lawless liberty—but that entirely—to rediscover his general freedom, undiminished, in dependence upon the law, i.e. in a condition of obedience to the law, because this dependence springs from his own lawgiving will.

It was Kant's deepest conviction that all men were entitled by nature to equal human rights, and that each member of society must accept such limitations of his rights and liberty as were demanded for the co-existence of the equally wellfounded freedom of his fellow-citizens.

The necessary conditions of citizenship are: statutary freedom, legal equality and civil independence.

Freedom, as the original right of every man, means: 'No one can force me to be happy in a manner which he thinks appropriate to the well-being of others, but everyone can seek happiness along the path which seems best to himself, so long as he

[1] *Complete Works of Kant*, Academy Edition, vol. vii, p. 85 f.

does not interfere with the liberty of others to pursue the same aim.'

Equality is the immediate consequence of liberty. From this idea of the equality of men in their common identity as subjects. is derived the formula: 'Every member of the same must be allowed to attain to that station therein, to which his talent, his industry and his good fortune may bring him.'

'The citizen's independence is his right, by virtue of his participation in public legislation. Every right is dependent upon laws. But a public law, determining for all what is legally permitted or forbidden, is an act of the public will, the source of all justice, which must be incapable of doing injustice to anyone. This condition can only be satisfied by the will of the whole nation; for it is only to himself that a person is incapable of doing injustice.'[1]

Legislative authority is vested in the united will of the people, which is the source of all justice. Every state comprises three authorities, namely supreme authority (sovereignty) in the hands of the legislator, executive authority in those of the ruler (by virtue of the law) and administrative authority in the person of the judge. The union of these three authorities constitutes the prosperity of the state (*salus rei publicae suprema lex est*),[2] which, however, does not imply the welfare and happiness of the citizens; for they, as Rousseau also states, might be much more comfortably circumstanced in a state of nature or even under a despotic régime. The concordance of the constitution with the principles of justice must be determined by the categorical imperative, the ethical will and practical reason, irrespective of outward happiness. Kant's ideal state is thus the constitutional state as demanded by the categorical imperative.

According to Kant's view, a true republic can be nothing else than a system representative of the nation and aimed at the protection of its rights, in its collective name and through the medium of its elected deputies . . . ; for the nation is the source of the highest authority, from which all the individual's rights

[1] ibid., vol. viii, p. 290 ff.
[2] The welfare of the state is the highest law.

must be derived. The essence of any régime ought to consist in everyone being able to provide for his own happiness and being free to combine with others to this end. It is not part of the government's task to relieve citizens of this concern, but only to create the prerequisites for it, while respecting the law of equality. Liberty must be preserved.

Of course, the objection that the people are not ready for liberty is frequently encountered. But on this presupposition, opines Kant, liberty would never be achieved; for a nation cannot become ready for freedom, if it is never set free. 'The first attempts', he writes, 'will naturally be crude, generally involving a situation of greater difficulty and danger than that in which men were subject to the orders, but also to the care, of others; there is no other way of becoming ready to live by reason than by one's *own* attempts to do so, to make which one must be free. I am in no way opposed to the belief that contemporary circumstances make it necessary for those in authority to postpone the liberation of the people for some considerable time. But to make it a principle that those who have once been in a subservient position are totally incapable of liberty, and that those in authority are justified in permanently withholding it from them, is an infringement of the prerogatives (sovereign rights) of the Godhead himself, who created men to freedom.'

True politics must always be made to conform to justice, justice must never be made to fit politics. True politics cannot take any step not previously sanctioned by morality. At whatever sacrifice to itself, the ruling authority must hold the rights of men sacrosanct. 'There is no room here for half-measures and compromise between justice and advantage; the whole of politics must bend the knee to justice, but in return it may hope to attain, though slowly, to the level at which it will shine with a constant light.' These statements of Kant's are marked by a clear formulation of the inalienable rights of man.

Even more sweeping are Kant's views on international relations, as set down in the previously mentioned essays on *Theory and Practice* (1793) and *Perpetual Peace* (1795).

It was not external events, such as military incidents, that gave

Kant the incentive to write *Perpetual Peace*,[1] which may be described as his political testament. It was a question of applying to the community of nations the ideas expounded in his *Critique of Practical Reason* (ethics). Already at the conclusion of his essay on *Theory and Practice* he had taken up problems of foreign policy: 'Nowhere does human nature present a less pleasant spectacle than in the relations of nations as a whole with one another. No state is for a moment safe from the others, in respect of its independence or its property. The will to subjugate or encroach upon others is always there, and preparations for defence, which often render peace even more burdensome and destructive of internal welfare than war itself, can never slacken. The only possible counter-measure to this state of affairs is international justice, founded upon public laws, to which every state must submit; for the maintenance of universal peace by means of the so-called Balance of Power in Europe is—like Swift's house, which a master-builder constructed in such perfect accord with all the laws of equilibrium, that when a sparrow alighted upon it, it immediately collapsed—a mere figment of the imagination.'[2]

Kant is not concerned to give the heads of states practical advice as to how war may be avoided. But as an idea, an ideal, his eyes are fixed upon a peaceful and free confederation of free states; he therefore turns to the politician's statecraft, and investigates the relationship of politics to morality.

The categorical imperative of duty, ethical consciousness, the voice of conscience must come to dominate politics, just as it must civic life. Politics must not pay homage to opportunism, there must be no contradiction between politics and morality, politics must not be a doctrine of astute manœuvre, but practical jurisprudence. Kant can envisage a moral politician, i.e. one who interprets the principles of statecraft in such a manner that they can be co-existent with morality, but not a political moralist, who moulds his morality into the shape which best fits the statesman's advantage.

---

[1] Second edition, 1796.
[2] *Complete Works of Kant*, Academy Edition, vol. viii, p. 312.

A state of peace cannot be expected from the nature of man; for malevolence is deeply rooted therein. It produces the state of war; even in the absence of an actual outbreak of hostilities, they threaten unceasingly. Thus, from a latent state of war, war itself finally emerges again and again. Within the state, the evil in men is veiled or suppressed by the compulsion of civil law, but in the external relations between states it comes into the open, unmasked and incontrovertible.

Peace, Kant calls that condition to which politics founded upon ethical freedom tend, just as political cunning, rooted in human malevolence, tends to the condition of war.

There were and are pacifists of another kind, such as Tolstoy and the representatives of Christianity, who dream of the kingdom of God upon earth and hope to establish peace among nations by means of Christian charity. Not so Kant! His idea of peace is not based on Christian love, but upon *law*. The constitution of a state should not be confined to the relations between the individuals within it, but must also include the state's own contacts with other states, which must rest upon the notion of law. Kant's eyes are fixed upon a kingdom of justice. Like Plato, he is of the opinion that political principles must proceed, not from the welfare and happiness which a state can expect to accrue, but from the pure concept of legal duty, from moral obligation, whose principle is given by pure reason *a priori* (duty, conscience), the consequences be what they may. Thus, just as the civil conduct of the individual should be unaffected by considerations of advantage or disadvantage, so the decisive factor in political conduct should be solely the sense of right, the voice of the categorical imperative, of conscience.

The fate of the citizen of a state depends, not only upon the internal organization of the state, but also upon its inter-relationship with other states; but Kant regards the notion of morality as unthinkable, so long as states employ their energies to forcible expansion. A state is not an isolated organism, but is in a position of close reciprocity with other states, which affects both its foreign and its domestic policy. The best guarantee of perpetual peace is the well-integrated constitutional state, such as is found in a republic. In this latter, legislative authority is separated from executive and vested in the whole population.

In the republican state, the actions of the government rest upon the will of the people. Thus war can only be waged with its consent. If the acquiescence of the *people themselves*, and not merely of their *representatives* in parliament, is required for a declaration of war, there will never be another war. No nation will be willing to take upon itself the sufferings of a war. Here Kant naturally presupposes popular sovereignty *throughout the whole family of states*; otherwise, the right of a nation to make its own decisions on peace or war might place it in grave danger. It is, of course, necessary, affirms Kant, for the individual republic to form part of the world-republic. The safeguarding of world peace ultimately depends upon the relations of the citizens of the various states with each other, as well as their relations with other states, being regulated by law. Kant castigates the mendacity of diplomacy in speaking of the conclusion of peace, when at best there is a temporary truce. The right of nations is taken to be a 'right to warfare'.

Kant is well aware that the notion of future permanent peace will be regarded as Utopian, and not taken seriously. But he hopes that it may prove possible gradually to establish the rule of law, from which perpetual peace might follow. For the time being, therefore, we are confronted with the task and duty of striving for this state of affairs, this political ideal. In spite of all previous catastrophic attempts to reach a settlement by war, the notion of law and the consciousness of having broken the law have survived. Unfortunately, the supremacy of the present powers still rests upon force, and it is not to be expected that, without more ado, 'right will come before might'; but it ought to be so.

One can do no more than work for a slow, but continual approximation to this political ideal. The ultimate goal seems to Kant to be a free association of free peoples, and in his *Jurisprudence* (1797) he puts forward the suggestion of a permanent congress of states endowed with powers of arbitration. This idea, though as yet in only a very modest degree, reached realization in the setting up of the United Nations Organization in San Francisco.

Kant's Postulates

1. *No peace ought to be accepted as such: if its conclusion is accompanied by the secret preservation of the material for a future war.*

For it would then be a mere truce, a postponement of hostilities, but not a real peace which means the end of all hostilities

2. *No state ought to be able to acquire another autonomous state (irrespective of whether it be great or small) by inheritance, exchange, purchase or gift.*

A state is not (like the ground on which it rests) a possession. It is a community of people, which ought to be at the command and disposal of no one but itself. But to graft him who, as an independent trunk, has his own roots, on to another state, means to deprive him of his moral existence and convert him into an object; it therefore controverts the idea of the original contract, without which no right over a nation is conceivable.

3. *Standing armies ought, in time, to be entirely abandoned.*

For they constitute a continual threat of war to other states, through the appearance of permanent military preparedness. If they incite others to embark upon an attempt to place an even greater number of men under arms, a process which has no limits, the consequent costs of peace may become more crushing than a short war; they themselves then become the cause of a war being launched to get rid of this burden.

But for the citizens to engage voluntarily in periodical military exercises, for the purpose of safeguarding their country against attacks from outside, is quite a different matter.

4. *No national debts ought to be contracted in respect of external trade with other states.*

To borrow money in the interests of the national economy (for purposes of road-improvement, new settlements, etc.) is a permissible procedure. But, as a machine for manœuvre and counter-manœuvre amongst the powers, a credit-system gives to money a dangerous power, whose future proportions cannot be foreseen but which, in the present, threatens the requirement that debts should only be contracted on the basis of security and enables one state to accumulate funds for the conduct of a war, in excess of those available to others. . . . The resulting facility in conducting a war . . . is a serious impediment to perpetual peace. . . .

5. *No state ought to intervene forcibly in the constitution and government of another state.*

What justification can there be for such an action? The autonomy of a state ought not to be assailed.

6. *No state ought to allow itself to commit acts of warfare of such a kind as will make reciprocal confidence impossible when the time comes to make peace: such acts include: the setting to work of assassins and poisoners: breaking the terms of surrender and incitement to treachery within the enemy state.*

For somehow or other trust in the enemy's mental outlook must be preserved, even in the midst of war, because without this no peace could be concluded, and hostilities would develop into a war of extermination. War is no more than the sorry expedient, in a state of nature, of asserting one's rights by force.

These are what Kant calls the six 'preliminary articles' or preconditions, without which perpetual peace is impossible; they are intended to do away with the *immediate* causes of a war.

He adds to them the following three 'final articles', which eliminate the deeper reasons for war and propose arrangements calculated to bring about the prospect of a lasting peace. They run:

(a) *The civil constitution of every state ought to be republican.*

Apart from the purity of its origin in the limpid fount of equity, the republican constitution also has prospects . . . of bringing about perpetual peace. If the assent of the people is required for the decision as to 'whether there shall be war or not', they will very naturally hesitate to embark upon such an adventure, since it would involve the decision to submit themselves to all the miseries of war.

(b) *International law ought to be based on a federation of free states.*

This idea of a federation, spreading gradually over all states and thus leading to perpetual peace, is not altogether unthinkable. For if good fortune ordains that a powerful and enlightened nation shall constitute itself a republic (which must, by its very nature, be disposed to perpetual peace), this will provide other states with a focus of federal union, to which they can attach themselves so as to ensure national liberty in conformity with the idea of international law. Further unions of the same kind will produce a continual expansion of the area of federation.

(c) *The rights of world-citizenship ought to be confined to the provisos of universal hospitality.*

Here, as in the previous articles, it is not a question of philanthropy, but of *rights*. In this context, hospitality[1] means the right of unmolested entry into a foreign country. As long as the visitor conducts himself in a peaceable manner, he ought not to be treated with hostility. It does not confer the right to demand accommodation, but merely to enter the country, to which all men are entitled by virtue of the common ownership of the surface of the earth.

Since the (close or broad) community of the peoples of the earth has already attained a degree of expansion, at which a violation of rights in *one* part of the earth is felt in *all*, the idea of world-citizenship rights is no fantastic exaggeration of the general conception of human rights. On the contrary, it is a necessary addition to the unwritten code of national and international law, essential to the rights of man as a whole and, hence, to perpetual peace. Only if the rights of world-citizenship become an established fact, can we flatter ourselves that we are drawing continually closer to this latter.

Thus 'perpetual peace' proves to be a political ideal, and according to Kant it is the duty of all heads of states, statesmen and citizens, by their intercession, to bring this ideal gradually nearer.

---

[1] From the Latin *hospes*, host or innkeeper. In this context, hospitality does not mean the right to be accommodated as a guest in a foreign country, but only the right to visit and reside in it. Kant expressly indicates that this is not a question of philanthropy, but of a duty imposed by rights.

9

Kant on Education

AMONGST THE SUBJECTS on which Kant lectured was 'Physical Geography'. On account of the abundance of material, he split off from it 'Anthropology', which he introduced as a separate subject from the Winter Session 1772-3 onwards, and in which he spoke in an arresting manner on the knowledge and observation of human nature. In the second part of this course, he gave an outline of 'Education'.

Kant's theoretical interest in questions of pedagogy had been especially aroused by the study of Rousseau's *Emile*. It is recounted that Kant, who, in later life adhered pedantically to a daily programme, became so absorbed in this novel, that it caused him to miss his habitual walk on the one and only occasion on which this happened. 'I must go on reading Rousseau', the philosopher once stated, 'until the beauty of his language ceases to interfere with the capacity of my reason to judge him.' And on another occasion: 'The first impression that a reader obtains from the writings of J. J. Rousseau is that he combines exceptional perspicacity, the noble ardour of genius and a depth of feeling to an extent probably unparalleled in any other writer.' Kant is particularly enthusiastic about the idea of re-establishing man's genuine, unadulterated nature, and the thesis that man has to learn, above all, how to be his natural self. Rousseau moved him to the declaration, very uncharacteristic of his way of thinking: 'Nothing great was ever achieved in this world without enthusiasm!'

In consequence of his interest in Rousseau, Kant paid great heed and gave his backing to the educational enterprises of Johann Bernhard Basedow (1724-90), who cherished the idea of a sweeping reform of upbringing and instruction in the direction

123

of Rousseau's theories. In 1774, Basedow had set up in Dessau a 'philanthropin', or school of human brotherhood, in which the essential educational principles of the great French teacher were to be put into practice. On the 28th March 1776 an anonymous appeal, written by Kant, was published in the *Königsberg Academic and Political Gazette* calling for active support of the Philanthropin in the form of money and pupils, so that 'this educational institution, which is equally well adapted to the purposes of nature and of society—the fruition of centuries of cogitation by brains of all qualities—shall expand and scatter its seed over other countries, which may bring about a great and sweeping reform of public and private life'. On the same day, Kant informed the principal of the Dessau Philanthropin that it was the wish of Mr. Motherby (his friend Green's partner) to entrust to the institution as a boarder his not yet six-years-old son, who, as the following remarks show, had hitherto been brought up in complete accordance with Rousseau's theories. 'His education so far has been purely negative, the best, in my belief, that could have been given at his age. His nature and sound intelligence have been permitted to develop, free from compulsion, in a manner appropriate to his years. There has been no interference beyond the removal of all influences capable of imparting a false direction to the development of his mind. He has received a free upbringing, but is not troublesome. He has never been harshly treated and quickly responds to mild remonstrance. In order to preserve his candour and avoid any occasion for lying, it has been preferred to condone a few childish faults.' In matters of religion, the father was in such close accord with the principles of the Philanthropin that the little boy had 'as yet, no idea of what devotional practices are'. He is only to be introduced to these after the natural recognition of God, which will come to him naturally 'with increasing years and understanding', has previously taught him that all such practices are merely a means of animating *active* piety and conscientious observance of *duties as divine commandments*. Here Kant was giving expression to views which he later set down in exactly similar terms in his book, *Religion within the Limits of Reason Alone* (1793).

In his lectures on anthropology, Kant continually sought to inspire his hearers with enthusiasm for the educational principles of Rousseau and Basedow; he called the Philanthropin 'the greatest phenomenon' of the century, in relation to the improvement of mankind. He made unceasing efforts, even after Basedow's death, to see that the Institute, which was always short of money, should receive increased funds for the support of young people, who came to it for two years' training in its methods and then returned home as educational reformers.

Kant's treatise *On Pedagogy* was written, in the form in which we know it, either in the years 1783-4 or 1786-7. He gave his last lecture on this discipline in the winter session 1786-7, so that his final addenda must date from this period. He did not publish the booklet himself, but left this to his former hearer and subsequent colleague Friedrich Theodor Rink, who did so in 1803, a year before Kant's death.

Kant drew his ideas on education from his seven years' experience as a teacher, together with his observation of life and the two writers whose work he most valued, Montaigne and Rousseau. His essay is a mine of acute reflections on educational psychology. But its reading will be more of a 'useful entertainment, than a burdensome task'; it consists pre-eminently of valuable practical advice on teaching as a profession.

Kant's views on education are not always consistent with the basic ideas and principles of his philosophy; they are characterized by the adoption of an *empirical* standpoint, which proves particularly fruitful and valuable in this domain. In his ethical writings, Kant has in mind the adult, who is possessed of autonomy, i.e. voluntary self-determination, and can be guided in his conduct by reason. But the child is a being in a state of becoming, of evolution, he is not yet ethically free and cannot yet take guidance from his reason.

In Kant's view, education is the greatest and most difficult problem than can confront a man. It is *invariably* a problem, i.e. an unresolved task. But why is it such a difficult undertaking? Education always involves a trinity, the child, the educator, who directly affects the child, and the whole of the child's environment, which exercises an unintentional influence upon it. But each of these three factors is a highly complex quantity, the child and the educator in their greatly differentiated predispositions, and then life, i.e. the whole motley multiplicity of fortuitous influences. The great diversity of the three factors named results in an infinite variation as between individual cases. Hence there can be no schema for education; every case is different, each case presents its own special difficulties, each case is a problem on its own, which must be solved in its own way.

Kant admits the *possibility* of education and is at the same time convinced of its necessity. At the pinnacle of his exposition he sets the proposition: 'Man is the only creature which has to be educated.' Kant does not base the necessity of education on any detailed analysis of human nature. For him, it emanates from the antithesis between man and beast. In Kant's view, man possesses the ability to set himself aims and goals and to cultivate the raw potentialities of his nature. The animal has only instinct, the gift of an alien reason. But man must learn to employ his own reason, and to this purpose education is necessary. Indeed, man can only become man through education and is nothing but what education, in the broad sense, makes of him. 'Behind education is concealed the great arcanum of the perfection of human nature.' If education continually improves, and each successive generation takes a further step forward, this will open up the vista of a future race of men, happier than the present. From the careful application of education throughout several generations, Kant hopes for a perfecting of human nature, of the genus Man.[1] Belief in the progressive perfecting of man was a favourite notion of the period. Lessing, Herder and Schiller dealt with it, while Fichte and Pestalozzi endeavoured to place it on a philosophic foundation.

As a convinced follower of Rousseau, Kant attaches great importance to healthy physical development, supporting natural

---

[1] The findings of modern experimental investigations into heredity have so far disproved the possibility of the inheritance of *acquired* characteristics. Nor is it conceivable in what manner educational measures could affect the germ-plasm.

diet and self-hardening procedures. From a mental point of view, the prime task is the moral development of man into a personality capable of self-determination based on reason. But the first stage is to 'discipline', i.e. 'civilize' man by the early combatting of his animal instincts. He must learn to inhibit himself; the most important means to this end are habituation and education to obedience. *Work* seems to Kant to be one of the best means of discipline. A propensity to slothfulness is a greater evil to man than anything else in the world. Children must learn to work and be accustomed to work from their very earliest years. 'Man is the only animal that has to work,' states Kant. Habituation to regular work begins in the school, which must look upon this as one of its foremost educational tasks. Kant opposes the current endeavours of the Philanthropinists to turn work into a caricature of play and to practise play-teaching. He discriminates strictly between play and work and wishes the difference to be kept clearly in view. Work-activity has no need to be pleasant in itself; it is undertaken for quite another purpose. But play is an occupation pleasurable in itself, carried on for its own sake and not to any ulterior end. Failure to discriminate clearly between work and play is, therefore, a pedagogic error.

The pupil must have time for recreation, but there must also be times for serious work. Habituation to work seems to Kant particularly necessary because of man's pronounced natural tendency to inactivity; the longer a man has idled, the more difficult he finds it to make up his mind to work.

It is self-evident that Kant entered in particular detail into the question of ethical education; for it is the most important part of practical education. The true vocation of man consists in the evolution towards morality, towards the moral character, whose whole conduct is guided by good principles. Initially, the young person takes these over uncritically from his home environment and from the school; but they must gradually become subjective laws, stemming from and sanctioned by reason. Man ought to develop such an attitude of mind that he only selects good aims. Good aims are those which must win the approval of everyman, and which it is desirable that everyman should adopt as his own, or, as Kant says elsewhere: Act in such a manner that you can wish the principles of your conduct to become the basis of universal legislation.

For the years of childhood, Kant naturally admits emotional reasons for moral conduct, such as sympathy, delight in good, distaste for evil. In his pedagogy, drawn from experience, Kant does not put forward such an austere interpretation as in his ethic. But in the mature adult, moral conduct must proceed from a sense of duty, from the categorical imperative, not from an emotional attitude.

According to Kant, the foundations of character-formation are education to *obedience*, to *veracity* and to *sociality*. To begin with, absolute obedience must be imposed, to be replaced later by voluntary obedience springing from the person's own reflection. Education to obedience is of extreme importance to character formation; for he who has not learnt to obey others is later unable to obey himself, his own convictions.

The second basic precondition for character formation, according to Kant, is *veracity*. 'A man who lies has no character at all, and if he has some good in him, this emanates solely from his temperament (disposition).' Character consists precisely in absolute unity of the personality; true character formation is rendered impossible by lies or inner contradictions.

The third characteristic, *sociality*, friendliness, makes children frank and merry. 'Only the joyful heart is capable of delighting in good.'

The principal means at the disposal of character formation are *example* and *precept*. As a means of imparting precepts, Kant recommends a 'Catechism of Right', which should deal in a universally intelligible form with cases from practical existence. Such a book would promote the moral development and education of children. The way in which Kant envisages such a Catechism of Right he shows by the following examples intended to be typical of its contents:

'If a man who is due to pay his creditor to-day is moved by the sight of another's want, and gives him the sum which he owes and is now due to pay, is that right or not? No! It is wrong;

for to carry out benefactions I must be free. And if I give money to the poor I am performing an act of merit, but if I pay my debt I am performing an act of duty.

'Further, is it permissible to lie out of necessity? No, under no conceivable circumstances can there be any excuse for a lie, least of all in the case of children, who would regard the slightest occasion as one of necessity and permit themselves to lie frequently.'

In accordance with his own nature, Kant's conception of ethical education has a strongly intellectual basis; its point of departure is rational insight into ethical facts. Religious instruction falls within the province of ethical education. As explained earlier, Kant's view of religion is a morality applied to the recognition of God. For this reason, religious education and instruction should not begin until late, otherwise religion becomes a mere 'currying favour'. 'Glorifications, prayers and church-goings have no purpose but to instil fresh strength, fresh courage to self-improvement, or to serve as the expression of a heart imbued with the idea of duty. They are only preparations to good deeds, not good deeds in themselves; there is no other way of pleasing the Most High save by becoming a better man ...'

In Kant's opinion, religious instruction must not consist merely in memorizing. God should be represented to children as the Lord of life and of the whole world, as man's provider and his highest judge.

Kant's basic pedagogic conviction is that education cannot achieve real success as long as it is carried on without a definite plan and merely proceeds from the situation of the moment. He takes the view that pedagogy must become a science, and if he did not himself raise it to this status, it is nevertheless of importance that such an ascendant spirit as Kant has made known his personal views on the subject, based on his abundant experience of life, and has given us valuable stimulation to their practical application.

10

Appreciation of Kant

KANT USHERED IN a new epoch in philosophical thought. His major writings constitute a milestone in the history of philosophy; he is one of those great and profound thinkers who, by their works, but also by their lives, exercised a lasting influence upon the intellectual life of their own time and posterity. No one concerned with philosophy can pass by his theories, whose further development continues to this day; he is compelled to come to terms with this 'critic who grinds everything to powder'.

F. Hebbel called him a thinker who moved and shook the world much more forcibly than his contemporary, Frederick the Great, with all his cannon.[1]

How extraordinarily important was Kant's effect upon Schiller, is well known. In a letter dated 13th June 1794, the latter assured him of his gratitude 'for the beneficent light which you kindled in my mind, a gratitude which is boundless and imperishable'.[2]

Admittedly, Kant's views are not satisfactory in all parts; they exhibit gaps and contradictions, which have led to their further elaboration from various quarters. But in a certain respect his ideas will remain the foundation of all philosophy. Indestructible is his recognition that the human mind is a creative force, that it is vitally operative, that it forms and fashions, that the phenomenal world is a picture of our own designing, that the constitution of our minds and the spontaneity of our thought determine the world as it appears to us and that the human mind is not passive in its behaviour, not a mere receptive vessel.

[1] Emil Kuh, *Friedrich Hebbel*, vol. ii, p. 438.
[2] *Kant's Correspondence*, Academy Edition, vol. ii, p. 488.

Of particular importance is his high valuation of moral duties and the emphasis he places on the dignity of man. The vital essence of his practical philosophy is his advocacy of active morality, loyal, undeviating, selfless devotion to duty and god-fearing belief in the good and divine. He established peace between knowledge and faith, assigning to each its own realm. Highly as he valued critical science, he well knew that it cannot explain everything and that faith too has its justification.

Kant's doctrines stand in the closest relationship to his life and personality, much more so probably than with other philosophers. Goethe had reached this insight when, in a conversation with J. D. Falk,[1] he remarked:

'Kant's strict moderation demanded a philosophy in conformity with his innate tendencies. Read his life, and you will soon find how agreeably he took the edge off his stoicism, which was, in fact, in sharp contrast to social conditions at the time, adjusted it and brought it into balance with the world.'[2]

How true! Kant's personal life and his philosophy form a unity. He was more than a great philosopher, he was a transcendent ethical personality, whose convictions had their centre of gravity in his constant and noble character. He determined his life from within himself, living what he taught.

[1] Falk, Johannes Daniel (1768–1826), writer, who lived in Weimar from 1798 until his death and belonged to the circle of Goethe's more intimate friends.

[2] *Goethe's Conversations*, published by W. Biedermann, vol. iv, p. 344 f., Leipzig, 1889.

Chronological List of Kant's Works

1746
Thoughts on the True Estimation of Living Forces.

1754
Investigation of the Question as to whether the Rotation of the Earth on its Axis has undergone any Modifications.

The Question as to whether the Earth is Growing Old, considered from the Angle of Physics.

1755
General Natural History and Theory of the Heavens, or an Attempt to Explain the Composition and Mechanical Origin of the Universe on Newtonian Principles.

1756
History and Natural Description of the Earthquake of 1755.

Consideration of recently perceived Earth-tremors.

Some Remarks towards Elucidation of the Theory of the Winds.

1758
A New Conception of Motion and Rest.

1759
Reflections on Optimism.

1762
The False Subtlety of the Four Syllogistic Figures.

1763
An Attempt to Introduce the Idea of Negative Magnitudes into Cosmology.

The Only Possible Proof of the Existence of God.

1764

Enquiry into Diseases of the Head.
Observations on the Sentiment of the Beautiful and the Sublime.

1766

Dreams of a Spirit-Seer, elucidated by the Dreams of Metaphysics.

1768

On the Primary Reason for the Distinction of Areas in Space.

1775

On the Various Races of Mankind.
Critique of Pure Reason.

1783

Prolegomena to Any Future Metaphysic which shall lay Claim to being a Science.

1784

Idea of a Universal History based on the Principle of World-Citizenship.
Response to the Question: What is Enlightenment?

1785

Concerning the Volcanoes on the Moon.
On the Illegality of Book-Pirating.
Definition of the Concept of a Human Race.
Fundamental Principles of the Metaphysic of Morals.

1786

Conjectures on the Beginnings of the History of the Human Race.
Learning How to Think.
Metaphysical First Principles of Natural Science.

1788

Critique of Practical Reason.

1790

Critique of Judgment.

Concerning a Discovery by which any Fresh Critique of Pure Reason may be rendered Superfluous by the Use of an Older One.

Concerning the Present Excess of Mystical Ecstasy and the Means of Remedying this Evil.

1791

Concerning the Possibility of a Theodicy and the Failure of all Previous Philosophical Attempts in this Field.

1792, 1793

On the Radical Evil in Human Nature in Religion within the Limits of Reason Alone.

On the Proverbial Saying: 'All Very Well in Theory, but no Good in Practice.'

1794

Something concerning the Moon's Influence on the Weather.

The End of All Things.

1795

Perpetual Peace; a Philosophical Project.

1797

Metaphysical First Principles of Jurisprudence.

Metaphysical First Principles of Moral Philosophy.

On a Supposed Philanthropic Justification for Lying.

1798

The Conflict of the Faculties, together with a treatise On the Power of the Mind to Master Morbid Feelings by Resolution Alone.

Anthropology from the Pragmatic Viewpoint.

1800

Logic, a Handbook for Lectures (edited by Jäsche).

1802

Physical Geography (edited by Rink).

1803

Kant on Pedagogy (edited by Rink).

Some Recent English Translations of Kant's Works

Perpetual Peace. Peace Book Co., London, 1939.

The Fundamental Principles of the Metaphysics of Ethics, translated with an introduction by Otto Mauthey-Zorn. D. Appleton-Century Co., New York; London, 1938.

The Moral Law; or, Kant's Groundwork of the Metaphysics of Morals. A new translation with analysis and notes by H. J. Paton. Hutchinson's University Library, 1948.

Critique of Pure Reason. J. M. Dent & Sons, London. (Everyman's Library, 1934.)

Critique of Pure Reason, translated by F. Max Müller. The Macmillan Company, New York.

Critique of Judgment, translated by J. H. Bernard. The Macmillan Company, New York.

Religion within the Limits of Reason Alone, translated by Theodore M. Greene and Hoyt H. Hudson. Open Court Publishing Company, Chicago.

Critique of Practical Reason and Other Works on the Theory of Ethics, translated by Thomas K. Abbott. Longmans, Green & Co., London.

Bibliography of English Works on Kant

Immanuel Kant: his life and doctrine, F. Paulsen (John C. Nimmo, London, 1902).

Student's Introduction to Critical Philosophy, etc., A. Weir (Joseph Thornton & Son, London, 1906).

The Philosophy of Kant Explained, John Watson (James Maclehose & Sons, Glasgow, 1908).

The Critical Philosophy of Immanuel Kant, Edward Caird, 2nd edition (James Maclehose & Sons, Glasgow, 1909).

Kant's Theory of Knowledge, H. A. Pritchard (Oxford University Press, 1909).

Moral Action and Natural Law in Kant, and some developments, E. M. Miller (George Robertson & Co., Melbourne, 1911).

Immanuel Kant, a Study and a Comparison with Goethe, Leonardo da Vinci, Bruno, Plato and Descartes, Houston Stewart Chamberlain; translated from the German by Lord Redesdale (John Lane, the Bodley Head, London, 1914).

A Study on Kant, James Ward (University Press, Cambridge, 1922).

An Introduction to Kant's Philosophy, Norman Clark (Methuen & Co., London, 1925).

Kant's Philosophy of Religion, Clement C. J. Webb (Clarendon Press, Oxford, 1926).

A Commentary on Kant's Critique of Pure Reason, Norman Kemp Smith (Macmillan, London, 1950).

Moral Law and the Highest Good. A study of Kant's doctrine of the highest good, E. M. Miller (University of Melbourne Publications No. 11, 1928).

Immanuel Kant in England 1793–1838, R. Wellek (Princeton University Press, 1931).

BIBLIOGRAPHY

Kant, Alexander D. Lindsay (Ernest Benn, Leaders of Philosophy, London, 1934).

Kant's Metaphysic of Experience. A Commentary on the first half of the Kritik der reinen Vernunft, 2 vols., Herbert J. Paton (George Allen & Unwin Ltd., London, 1936).

A Short Commentary on Kant's Critique of Pure Reason, Alfred C. Ewing (Methuen & Co., London, 1938).

A Commentary on Kant's Critique of Judgment, H. W. Cassirer (Methuen, London, 1938).

Morality and Freedom in the Philosophy of Immanuel Kant, William Tudor Jones (O.U.P., Oxford Classical and Philosophical Monographs, London, 1940).

The Living Thoughts of Kant, presented by Julien Benda (Cassell & Co., Ltd., Living Thoughts Library, London, 1942).

The Categorical Imperative. A study of Kant's moral philosophy, Herbert J. Paton (Hutchinson's University Library, London, 1947).

(Compiled by the translator)

Index

INDEX

INDEX

Hebbel, Friedrich, 130
Héloise, 37
Heraclitus, 39
Herder, 36, 126
Herz, Marcus, 31, 52
Hippel, G. R. von, 55
Hippel, Theodor Gottlieb von, 19, 30, 40, 42
Hope, 105
Hülsen, Bernhard Friedrich von, 23 f.
Human dignity, 103
 nature, 126
Hume, 37, 39, 79
Hypochondria, 52

Imagination, 84
Immanuel Kant, 28
Immanuel Kant as seen through letters to a friend, 16
Immanuel Kant during the last years of his life, 64
Immortality, 87, 89
Improvement of Women's Position in Society, 40
Independence, civil, 114 f.
Inference, 88
Instincts, 93, 126
Insterburg, 23
Intelligence, 95
Intuition, 82

Jachmann, Reinhold Bernhard, 16, 34, 36, 39, 41, 43, 46, 49, 51, 53, 61, 106
Jacobins, 113
Jacobism, 67
Jensch, Police Superintendent, 63
Joachimsthal Grammar School, 23 f.
Judgements, 81
Judtschen, 23
Justice, 114, 116

Kant, Barbara (Kant's sister), 58

Kanter, 28 ff.
Kant in Old Age, 59
Kant, Johann Georg (Kant's father), 15, 20
Kant, Johann Heinrich (Kant's brother), 56 ff.
Kant, Maria Elisabeth (Kant's sister), 57
Kant's Correspondence, 130
Kepler, 37
Königsberg, 15, 17, 20, 27, 36
 University, 20 ff., 24, 26, 31 f., 37, 53, 73
Knutzen, Martin, 21
Körner, Theodor, 97
Kuh, Emil, 130

Lampe, Martin, 59, 62 ff.
Laplace, Pierre-Simon, Marquis de, 26

Latin, 18
 poetry, 53
Lavater, Johann Caspar, 46
Law, 114
Lectures, public, 35
Legislation, 115
Leibniz, 37, 39, 79
Leiden, 19
Lessing, 42, 126
Letters on Kantian Philosophy, 70
Letters on the Advancement of Humanity, 36
Liberty, 114 ff.
Lie, 129
Lienhard and Gertrud, 97, 107
Locke, John, 39, 54, 79 f.
Logic, 25
Loose Sheets from the Literary Remains, 113
Love, 110 f.
 Christian, 118
Lupin, Friedrich, 61 f.

INDEX